Published by
Edward Elgar Publishing Limited
The Lypiatts
15 Lansdown Road
Cheltenham
Glos GL50 2JA
UK

Edward Elgar Publishing, Inc.
William Pratt House
9 Dewey Court
Northampton
Massachusetts 01060
USA

A catalogue record for this book
is available from the British Library

Library of Congress Control Number: 2012952876

This book is available electronically in the ElgarOnline.com Business Subject Collection, E-ISBN 978 1 78100 552 1

ISBN 978 1 78100 551 4

Typeset by Columns Design XML Ltd, Reading
Printed by MPG PRINTGROUP, UK

Contents

Figures

Tables

Abbreviations

ARD	American Research and Development
BIC	Business Innovation Centre
CPI	Corporate Private Incubator
CVC	corporate venture capital
EU	European Union
GEM	Global Entrepreneurship Monitor
ICT	information and communications technology
IPI	Independent Private Incubator
IPO	initial public offering
IPR	intellectual property rights
IT	information technology
KIE	knowledge intensive entrepreneurship
KIS	knowledge intensive services
LSP	LEGO Serious Play™
M&As	mergers and acquisitions
MIT	Massachusetts Institute of Technology
NBIA	National Business Incubation Association
NGO	non-governmental organization
NTBF	new technology-based firm
NVCA	National Venture Capital Association
NVG	New Ventures Group
R&D	research and development
SBICs	Small Business Investment Companies
SMEs	small- and medium-sized enterprises
TBPM	tangible business process modelling
UBIs	University Business Incubators
UCSF	University of California at San Francisco
USOs	university spin-outs

Preface

This book is developed in a larger context in relation to the FP7 project, AEGIS –'Advancing Knowledge Intensive Entrepreneurship and Innovation for Economic Growth and Social Well-being in Europe', project contract number 225134. AEGIS aims to examine knowledge intensive entrepreneurship, its defining characteristics, boundaries, scope and incentives in high-technology as well as low-technology sectors and in services. The reports from this project are freely available, and constitute many papers with interesting results and insights about knowledge intensive entrepreneurship (KIE). We encourage the reader of this book to also seek out such knowledge at www.aegis-fp7.eu.

Special thanks to Ann McKinnon for her help and support in completing this book.

1. Introduction

1.1 INTRODUCTION

This book focuses on a particular type of entrepreneurship, called knowledge intensive entrepreneurship, shortened to 'KIE'. We start from the view that KIE phenomena can be found in many sectors such as low-tech industries, design firms, service firms and also in the traditionally studied areas like 'high-tech sectors' and 'academic spin-offs'. Naturally, the ideas presented here draw upon previous literature, not least within the field of technology-based ventures and academic entrepreneurship. However, existing studies primarily focus upon industries driven by opportunity creation in basic science and technology. This book goes beyond this to propose a new KIE creation model based on a richer understanding of the interactions between the KIE venture and the external environment for opportunities and knowledge.

One main message of this book is that entrepreneurship is a phenomenon that may be thought of as a structured and defined process, but also one involving uncertainty and risk due to the nature of knowledge involved. Concepts like uncertainty and risk mean that you don't know what will work or not. Will the idea sell and access financing? Will the technology work in the way you imagine? Is the creative idea something that can be realized in practice? Is anyone interested in purchasing and using the services? We know that many small firms will fail but a few succeed – for a shorter or longer period. One explanation may lie in the broader societal effects, which represent areas beyond the control of the individual or venture, and that is why the interactions between individuals, ventures (companies) and societal influences are of interest here. Our contributions are threefold in ways of interest to the readers.

This book first proposes a KIE creation model. This model structures our thinking and directs our attention to the key decision-points and processes. The KIE creation model provides a synthesis of the main phases and second-order variables. The model is applicable and useful for many purposes, including discussing societal impacts and the role of public policy, as well as managing companies.

The book also explains how this KIE creation model enables us to understand entrepreneurship as a structured and defined process, involving uncertainty in many dimensions. Planning is a useful tool. And yet entrepreneurship is also a process involving individuals, venture and societal influences. They create different domains of knowledge. Their interactions introduce the possibility to access resources and ideas but also introduce uncertainty, risk and the idea that ventures can fail.

Finally, our contribution is to apply the model and conceptualization of KIE to understanding the importance of different types of knowledge such as those found in low-tech industries, services and other areas of society like social entrepreneurship. Taken together, three types of knowledge relevant to KIE are: (1) scientific, technological and creative knowledge that leads to new ideas and opportunities; (2) market knowledge as related to the market and to customers and users; and (3) business knowledge as related to how to manage and structure internal firm processes. All three types of knowledge may involve uncertainty from the perspective of the KIE venture – what is known? Who wants potential products and services? And how can we organize to deliver it?

KIE is here defined as a particular type of start-up venture and phenomenon. We use the term 'KIE venture' for the company, business project or new organizational form created in this way as well as the concept of 'KIE' for the overall phenomenon and processes of this type of entrepreneurship. KIE phenomena reach beyond the mere establishment of a new venture, and have significant implications for societal growth and wealth creation. The KIE processes as we discuss them are highly dynamic with strong feedback loops between the individuals, the company and society.

Thirteen case studies can be found in the companion book, *How Entrepreneurs Do What They Do: Case Studies in Knowledge Intensive Entrepreneurship* (McKelvey and Lassen, 2013), also published by Edward Elgar. This book provides detailed information about specific firms and venture creation processes. The case studies cover many different kinds of firms and sectors, and they illustrate how and why KIEs develop and are managed over time. They discuss how new products and services are developed and often in situations where no customers already exist but instead where markets need to be formed. The case studies address very different types of firms, ranging from high-tech to low-tech to ones primarily providing services. Each case addresses specific questions and illustrates aspects of KIE phenomena.

Both books are relevant for many different kinds of readers, ranging from advanced students and practitioners such as venture capitalists, entrepreneurs and policy-makers, as well as for academics. The books provide a platform for discussing how to stimulate successful entrepreneurship as starting firms or as stimulating the KIE phenomena. Our approach has major implications for what we should learn about entrepreneurship, why public policy may intervene and how to engage practically in venture creation, making the books directly relevant to the library market as well as many types of readers.

Taken together, the two books are thus useful for understanding the 'doing' of creating ventures through this type of entrepreneurship, as illustrated through the cases and empirical insights as well as the 'knowing' related to structuring our understanding, as found in the KIE creation model, based upon an underlying conceptual framework

Let us now shift focus to our approach to understanding KIE as relevant to business and society. The next section defines a set of propositions, or our claims about what is particularly important to understand about KIE; the following section introduces this book, in terms of our approach. Both sections constitute our main message. The final section contains a summary of each chapter in order to provide a road map for readers, laying out the main ideas and results.

1.2 ABOUT KNOWLEDGE INTENSIVE ENTREPRENEURSHIP

The following seven statements, or propositions, are what this book is about, and they are discussed in the subsequent chapters. They help summarize what we mean in saying that this book aims to provide empirical evidence and theoretical insights.

These seven propositions are a way of summarizing the main points in this book. They also help explain the processes and phenomena, and causality, of what are admittedly complex economic and societal processes. They help place the individual and the company within a broader societal context and thereby how societal impacts and public policy influence what happens.

Our propositions are:

1. *KIE ventures represent special forms of venture creation and they are different from other types of entrepreneurship. Partly, there is a definitional issue of focusing upon that subset of firms that uses various types of knowledge and innovation as the key competitive asset, regardless of industry. However, the special form of venture creations also focuses on the relationships that occur between KIE venture creation and context, during different business phases.*

2.   *KIE is achieved through a series of decisions, which lead to the balancing of alternative logics between business planning and emergence of unexpected opportunities. A number of structures and variables are identifiable and must be considered when planning the development of a new company. These include elements within the company but also elements in the external ecosystem and environment. But the interpretation of such variables and how one acts upon them in a company will result in a variety of different outcomes. This underlies the evidence-based approach as well as the creative development of the venture.*

3.   *Accessing inputs, which are resources and ideas, is crucial to starting the company. This phase refers to the processes and phenomena before the venture is created, but also takes up subjects like financing that remain relevant during later management phases. The emphasis is on how and why to use resources and ideas that are linked to the founder, or which can be transferred from the ecosystem and external environment to the venture. This focus on inputs reflects the fact that KIE ventures rarely come out of the blue. Indeed, the KIE venture often draws upon existing organizations, and this leads to many decisions about how and why to use resources and relationships to balance planning and emergent opportunities.*

4.   *Significant differences exist between entrepreneurial management and general management. As one vital example, entrepreneurial management relies highly on the use of networks and emergence of access to resources. Therefore, management of KIE ventures requires a systemic understanding of processes and of the relationship between individual and context in order to design and carry out this type of entrepreneurship.*

5.   *Evaluating the performance and outputs of KIE and KIE ventures requires a more nuanced understanding of how KIE can drive innovation, growth and societal development. There are different measurement techniques, and a handful of indicators are often used but may be poor indications of the performance and outputs of KIE. Moreover, at the level of KIE ventures and of society, the performance measures should include a dynamic and systemic element, as they often undergo dramatic shifts over time.*

6.   *Our view is that design thinking can be developed and utilized to play an important role for the successful exploration and exploitation of KIE. Without this there is a lack of tools and techniques to manage tensions between creativity and order or structure. With*

this we can develop a systemic approach to shaping the thinking about venture creation and innovation for developing KIE ventures.

7. *A key issue is how and why to develop public policy and societal influences that are important for being able to explain, and stimulate, KIE processes and phenomena. The broader societal context explicitly affecting the development and formation of KIE ventures especially includes knowledge, markets, institutions and opportunities. Just as design thinking provides tools at the level of the KIE venture, public policy also has tools and recommendations about how to encourage and support this type of entrepreneurship.*

1.3 INTRODUCING THIS BOOK

Primarily, this book takes a managerial view on the process, running from opportunities, through strategies and internal management processes to outcomes and rewards for risk-taking behaviour. Thus, this book follows in the tradition of this field as outlined by Venkataraman (1997), among other authors and contributions, in understanding the nexus of enterprising individuals and valuable opportunities. However, this book pushes the analysis further than books on general entrepreneurship by our focus upon different types of knowledge and opportunities for interaction with society, and by introducing design thinking as a tool for managing these types of ventures.

The concept 'entrepreneurship' refers in a broader sense to KIE phenomena and processes. Research in entrepreneurship may well be a 'catch-all' term, and this type of research is carried out by scholars in many different disciplines (Davidsson et al., 2001). But what is interesting here is in what ways does the diversity of existing research help us develop an informed understanding of the processes?

Carlsson et al. (2012) provide a useful definition from our perspective, based upon a review of the major theoretical contributions in the field:

> Entrepreneurship refers primarily to an economic function that is carried out, by individuals, entrepreneurs, acting independently and within organizations, to perceive and create new opportunities and to introduce their ideas into the market, under uncertainty, by making decisions about location, product design, resource use, institutions, and reward systems. The entrepreneurial activity and the entrepreneurial ventures are influenced by their socio-economic environment, and they result ultimately in economic growth and human welfare.

This definition comes from a scientific paper, which takes the approach of outlining the main contributions and synthesizing many diverse strands of research. The authors undertake this review in order to present a more coherent explanation of entrepreneurship and to identify areas for future research.

Our theoretical perspective is also in line with a process view. The modern view is that entrepreneurial processes and logic should be seen as a balancing act between business planning under rationality and the messy reality of running a business venture. What happens over time is the emergence of unexpected opportunities and events that lead to new problems and new thinking that the business must make decisions about, and address consequences during management phases.

We would like to stress that the process of creating a KIE venture as conceptualized here defines entrepreneurship as a creative process rather than rote learning. The KIE venture is designed in order to respond to one or more innovative opportunities and these opportunities can emerge from things such as new technology, new markets and new ways of using internal and external resources. Creativity in this sense means that the entrepreneur, or founder, and their team and organization will have to always be balancing new ideas and ways of doing things against existing routines, the notion of efficient structures and set organizational routines. This type of balancing between multiple objectives and shifts in direction seem inherent to the process of delivering upon the ideas to realize new products and services.

We now turn to the discussion of our broader starting points:

- Framing KIE phenomena as one way of solving grand societal challenges, including the concerns of young people and government, like social innovation, environment and similar large issues.
- Specifying an evidence-based approach to learning about, engaging in and evaluating KIE.

1.3.1   Framing KIE Phenomena as One Way to Solve Grand Societal Challenges

A first topic is how we frame KIE phenomena as one way to solve grand societal challenges. The importance of KIE in society and the economy is a broad and complex topic, not always with clear-cut answers.

This type of entrepreneurship represents more general impacts on society. The specific definitions used in this book allow us to expand our analysis beyond 'high-tech' or 'research and development (R&D) intensive' firms and sectors to also encompass low-tech firms and services as well as social innovation and public service innovations. The concept thus represents a variety of business models and ways in which entrepreneurship takes place in society and the economy. Entrepreneurs need many types of knowledge and many different business models when they go about starting companies, selling products, licences and services, and thereby influencing society.

Thus, entrepreneurship takes on new importance in a knowledge economy because it serves as a key mechanism by which knowledge created in one organization becomes commercialized in a new enterprise.

Society faces grand societal challenges such as climate, ageing populations and the global use of current and future resources. These challenges were initially conceptualized as fairly long term, but the economic crisis in 2008 has also affected our ideas of 'development', and what public policy can do to affect unemployment, poverty and similar societal issues. Innovation and entrepreneurship are part of the solution through testing many ideas in an open manner.

These grand societal challenges are global, in the sense that people, organizations, non-governmental organizations (NGOs) and governments all over the world will have to deal with them. Yet how we find technologies, organizations and ways of working to reduce the problems will differ. Some solutions will be global, while other solutions will be local: some solutions will primarily involve business and others the government and public services; other solutions will involve civic society or the community.

The companion case study book suggests that there are many ways to organize the translation of opportunities and ideas into solutions that deliver innovations of use to society.

KIE will, in addressing these grand societal challenges, be one powerful organizational solution in bringing together people, resources and ideas in order to deliver things that society wants. There are related organizational solutions as well, such as large companies and social innovation run through non-profit or community means. This type of entrepreneurship does help introduce and stimulate dynamics in existing firms and sectors, often through novel technologies commercialized through a venture. There are also other ways, such as social entrepreneurship and base-of-the-pyramid or frugal innovation, which may be directly related to, or morph into, KIE ventures.

Empirical evidence suggests that KIE represents powerful mechanisms for growth and renewal. Some will succeed. Some will fail. Others will struggle along, with certain periods of success and other periods of failure. KIE ventures have therefore become the object of many policy-making efforts in recent years. The main conclusions of research are that KIE ventures that survive tend to grow faster, and stimulate growth.

These processes and phenomena help stimulate economic growth and societal well-being (from an overall perspective), given their role in generating new jobs, productivity and growth. Studies reaching these conclusions focus upon the importance of mechanisms like academic spin-offs and corporate spin-offs as well as impacts upon the region and industry.

We argue that KIE ventures are not confined to high-tech or new sectors, and that public policy needs to be developed in terms of goals and instruments, to impact low-tech sectors, manufacturing and existing industries. Moreover, a main area for innovation and entrepreneurship in coming years is the public sector, which will likely rely upon a combination of business and social innovations. Naturally, the discussion of social well-being is a complex one, as is the concept of economic growth.

This broader perspective is necessary because a vital issue for students and researchers, as well as policy-makers, is how to capture the dynamic effects and value created for society through entrepreneurship. Related key issues are what types of venture creation should be stimulated, how knowledge is translated into value and what types of policy goals and instruments are effective. We will not answer all these questions, but this book can help the reader understand the processes and apply new solutions to real problems. Understanding the overall phenomena is a necessary prerequisite to stimulate firms to solve the challenges facing society. Hence, we suggest that public policy can make a better impact if there is an understanding of the key processes and special characteristics of KIE ventures in society and the economy.

1.3.2　Specifying an Evidence-based Approach

Even though we stress an evidence-based approach and systemic results, this does not mean that this book is a traditional academic book, written for other professors. Nor does it rely upon a linear process model, but instead relies upon a more complex set of variables in a feed-back system model. For anyone wondering about whether our results are valid and reliable – or wondering how to do their own study, such as in a thesis – we explain what we mean by an evidence-based approach.

Learning involves finding out what other people have discovered, and hence one focus here is the literature review and our proposed KIE creation model. It represents a map, or conceptual framework, based on research results, because it can help identify concepts, processes, variables, cause and effects of venture creation, from a larger perspective.

Engaging in entrepreneurship requires doing and knowing. Both the entrepreneur and the reader interested in starting a firm will have to balance 'doing' and 'knowing'. By 'doing' we mean engaging practically in actual venture creation processes and by illustrations and case studies. Much of the knowledge relevant to one specific firm will be developed when the project developed and the firm was up and running. By 'knowing' we mean learning through specific empirical evidence and case studies as well as general knowledge and tools for evaluating processes and outcomes. Both 'doing' and 'knowing' are vital in helping the reader understand how and why they make good choices in practical action.

Then there is 'evaluating', which refers to being able to work with and identify productive processes of development like design thinking. Evaluating also refers to methods and techniques for evaluating performance and outcomes, generally using quantitative methods.

Thus, in talking about an evidence-based approach, this book draws on a vast academic literature, which tries to explain cause and effects and empirical process outcomes in a systematic way. If you only know what happened or was possible within a single case study interpreted by the practical entrepreneur, then you have no idea if the learning from that process can be applied to later ventures. These stories are important. They help us understand how the individual acted. Moreover, what is clear is that personal relationships (which are called networks and social capital) and experience matter, so that a person who has started a firm has valuable information useful to the next entrepreneur. However, we will not know if the founder happened to be skilful and lucky, and above all if there is similar learning to be had from other cases, industries and countries if we do not have more systematic evidence.

This book takes and uses an evidence-based approach to KIE ventures and this type of entrepreneurship. From the AEGIS project involving more than 30 partners, we use material developed through a survey across Europe as well as the more than 80 case studies that have been written. Material can be found on the AEGIS website http://www.aegis-fp7.eu.

Moreover, an evidence-base approach means that a substantial amount of scientific results have been condensed and synthesized here. Scientific results are generally published as peer-reviewed articles and books in order to check the validity and generalizability of the results (as well as guarantee an element of theoretical and/or empirical novelty). There is a particular way of working within sciences, including social sciences like business and economics, to try to make sure the demonstration of causality and outcomes is valid across more than one case. Peer review is one method for trying to guarantee quality, and it is used on published work but evaluation by experts is also used in the selection of which scientific projects to fund.

Much of science is also about defining taxonomies and special cases where theories have been tested and are held to apply – or to be irrelevant. A good reading about how scientific theories enable prediction and better action is 'Why hard-nosed executives should care about management theory' (Christensen and Raynor, 2003).

The reason we point this out is that scientific results about KIE ventures and this type of entrepreneurship, as reported in this book, are based upon a vast body of knowledge. The conceptual framework and the KIE creation model can be seen as resulting from a systematic way of working to try to explain what we know about the world around us – as opposed to speculation, individual interpretations and the like.

The background information comes from a systemic literature on our topic, which we later refined and developed into the KIE creation model. The Appendix describes the process of how to conduct such a literature review in general – as well as our specific choices. The book contributes through a systematic review of what works and what doesn't, and of what matters and what doesn't matter to these types of business ventures, in order to facilitate evaluation.

But if you want to develop it into a new model, then such a review should also include a critical understanding. This means trying to identify major dimensions and variables, and what causes what. By having a critical approach to methods, data and techniques, the reader can further develop his or her own understanding and approaches to learning about, engaging in and evaluating this type of entrepreneurship.

Thus, we feel that we make an important contribution, which is to develop a synthesis of the main phases and second-order variables. Essentially, we translate the findings systematically into a comprehensive unified conceptual framework focused upon the topics addressed.

The reader may also wish to impact society, and systemic evidence is needed here as well. You have the opportunity for learning by developing competencies, skills and techniques about KIE set within a reflective, critical approach to what is knowledge. The idea is that this combination of theoretical understanding with practical insights also matters for society. It will help in stimulating economic growth and societal well-being, beyond starting a business venture per se.

In summary, we can generate knowledge about KIE phenomena, drawing on case studies as well as quantitative data and from both empirical work and work that is primarily theoretical and conceptual. We synthesize and condense the results in a novel way in order to be able to say more about the processes, variables and outcomes of KIE ventures, seen as a business proposition.

STRUCTURE OF THIS BOOK

Chapter 2, entitled 'The knowledge intensive entrepreneurship creation model', defines the concept, addresses the special characteristics of KIE ventures and visualizes the model. The chapter explains our definition, which represents a novel concept, which can be useful to draw together research and also help structure decision-making. Taken together, three elements position our perspective and the type of entrepreneurship as different to the general entrepreneurship literature. Elements of our KIE creation model include a focus on:

- the specific role of different types of knowledge in entrepreneurship
- interactions between individuals and business ventures with the ecosystem and external context
- opportunities created and designed through these interactions with the ecosystem.

We define the processes and broader phenomena by explicit consideration of the main concepts, processes, variables, cause and effects, and by relating KIE ventures to a broader context (networks, innovation policy and public policy). This enables us to discuss the entrepreneur as well as the KIE venture and the ecosystem or external environment.

This definition then leads us to present the KIE creation model, which represents the underlying conceptual framework. The KIE creation model outlines three main phases of this type of entrepreneurship. These phases are: accessing resources and ideas; managing the venture; and assessing outputs and performance.

Chapter 3 is entitled 'Accessing resources and ideas'. The chapter addresses the origins of, and important inputs to, KIE and relates this to the broader ecosystem and societal context. The chapter focuses upon the third proposition, related to how accessing resources and ideas occurs in relation to emerging opportunities for KIE ventures, and that this process unfolds over time.

There are clear reasons why we start by discussing business founding, inputs and resources rather than focusing on the internal processes of business plans. One such reason is that modern entrepreneurship literature has found that the individual entrepreneur – or firm – relies upon inputs and resources from other actors in society, and we feel this is an interesting line of thought to further pursue. Moreover, the source, quality and type of inputs and resources tend to influence the success of these types of firms as much as the internal management processes functioning in the next phase.

We would like to point out that financing is vital but only one part of the understanding, and that different rounds of financing often play a key role, in changing the direction and even strategy of the firm. But the other issues may be as vital to understanding the firm.

Chapter 4 is entitled 'Managing and developing the knowledge intensive entrepreneurship venture'. Having discussed the inputs of KIE, the chapter focuses on the processes of maturing and managing the KIE venture, highlighting different dimensions of the management and development of this type of venture, that are particularly important. The chapter also addresses the fourth proposition, related to what it means that significant differences exist between entrepreneurial management and general management. Many KIE ventures struggle when trying to prioritize different types of knowledge. So, for example, in high-tech sectors, they struggle between different visions of the importance of technological knowledge versus market knowledge, and the same processes can be found in service or creative industries, where there is a struggle with creative knowledge. Usually, this leads to a discussion of 'maturing the venture', by which we refer to the transformation processes the venture undergoes and how interplay between internal and external sources is created to affect growth. Moreover, in making these arguments, we also briefly touch upon the converse, namely that entrepreneurial thinking also matters for existing organizations when they are trying to build innovative structures.

Chapter 5, 'Evaluating performance and outputs', focuses upon the third phase of KIE, that is, the outputs and performance of KIE ventures. To make progress in this discussion, we argue that it is necessary to have a developed understanding of:

- measuring techniques
- four indicators and measurements of KIE
- dynamic and systemic effects.

The main focus is upon evaluating performance through indicators and measurements of KIE. We first consider the trade-offs between quantitative and qualitative measuring techniques. Then we focus upon four indicators related to new firm formation, growth performance, patents, and knowledge creation.

In addition, this last issue of dynamic and systemic effects leads us to the discussion of evaluating the actual performance and outputs at the KIE venture and societal level. Related questions are: do these benefits only exist for the KIE venture created and the individual founder, or who becomes a millionaire? How and why does society benefit or carry the risks and costs? What types of effects should be expected and demanded by society? These are difficult but important issues, and the chapter will briefly introduce this overall discussion while the main focus is upon indicators and measurements.

Chapter 6 is entitled 'Design thinking as a tool for entrepreneurship'. We argue that design thinking plays an important role for the successful exploration and exploitation of KIE, and this is reflected throughout our discussions on how to navigate in the creation of KIE, and how different types of input to KIE enhance or decrease the likelihood of success.

Design thinking helps provide tools and techniques as part of a creative process. Starting a firm requires this combination of business inputs and resources, and many current authors use the concepts of opportunity recognition and mobilization to understand these processes. Therefore, in the specific case of KIE, opportunities can be seen as resulting from an emerging design process. Our concept of entrepreneurship is as a creative process, realizing the process and development of innovative opportunities in the context of a KIE venture.

Design thinking will be introduced in terms of a set of useful tools and techniques in this process of starting and developing a KIE venture. This is because it represents a way of thinking and working about how to deal with what you know and expect and can plan about, as well as how to deal with what you do not know, cannot predict and cannot plan about.

Chapter 7 is entitled 'Societal impacts of knowledge intensive entrepreneurship and the role of public policy'. The chapter concludes with critical reflections about the impacts of these processes and phenomena on public policy and society and thus addresses the sixth proposition about the broader impact of KIE on economic growth and social well-being, and how public policy can influence it. The broader context that we have defined as explicitly affecting the formation, management and performance of KIE ventures especially includes knowledge, markets, institutions and opportunities. Thus, the chapter also returns to our starting definition of entrepreneurship by providing novel insights related to public policy and society. Entrepreneurship is more than knowing how to build a company because it represents a line of thinking about how to shape business and society.

The Appendix proposes specific steps and goals for readers about how to undertake a literature review on similar topics. It includes a detailed overview of the methodology for our initial, systemic literature review, including an explanation of the choices we made. The Appendix also provides a detailed overview of the existing literature, including tables, which highlight the foci of existing empirical and theoretical studies.

2. The KIE creation model

2.1 INTRODUCTION

This chapter explains what we mean by these two propositions:

- *KIE ventures represent special forms of venture creation and they are different from other types of entrepreneurship. Partly, there is a definitional issue of focusing upon that subset of firms that uses various types of knowledge and innovation as the key competitive asset, regardless of industry. However, the special form of venture creations also focuses on the relationships that occur between KIE venture creation and context during different business phases.*
- *KIE entrepreneurship is achieved through a series of decisions, which lead to the balancing of alternative logics between business planning and emergence of unexpected opportunities. A number of structures and variables are identifiable and must be considered, when planning the development of a new company. These include elements within the company but also elements in the external ecosystem and environment. But the interpretation of such variables and how one acts upon them in a company will result in a variety of different outcomes. This underlies the evidence-based approach as well as the creative development of the venture.*

This chapter proposes our KIE creation model, and it consists of three phases with second-order variables and identification of key themes. The first phase has to do with accessing resources and ideas, which can be seen as a focus upon inputs and 'endowments' that already exist in the ecosystem. The entrepreneur and founding team may bring these with them into the start-up phase. The second phase is managing and developing these ventures. This has to do with how to organize and structure internal processes once the company is started and how to balance multiple objectives. The third phase has to do with defining performance, which is about how to measure and evaluate performance over time. Each phase has a specific set of variables that we shall address in subsequent chapters.

The next section provides the definition of KIE, followed by a discussion of three special characteristics that differentiate it from other types of entrepreneurship. The subsequent section presents the KIE creation model.

2.2 DEFINING KIE

It would be easier if we could define KIE as only occurring in certain industries – say, high-tech industries like biotechnology – or only occurring in certain types of firms – say, academic spin-offs. But we start from the view that KIE is a phenomenon that can be found in many sectors such as low-tech industries, design firms and service firms.

Definitions matter a lot, in this complex subject. We want to include interactions across different levels, because our argument is that the interactions matter. We use the term 'founder' or 'entrepreneur' for the individual; the term 'KIE venture' for the company or business project, as well as the concept of 'KIE' to represent the broader processes and phenomena for this type of entrepreneurship.

This book mainly focuses upon KIE venture creation as a management process. However, we are very aware of the importance of the external environment for things like finance, ideas and sales, so therefore we also discuss entrepreneurship as a broader set of processes and phenomena as well. Taking in these levels will enable us to discuss the relationships between how the individual acts and the decision-making for the company in relation to the broader business and societal context.

Following Malerba and McKelvey (2010), we rely upon a formal definition of KIE, also used in a very large European Union project (http://www.aegis-fp7.eu). This is used in the AEGIS survey and case studies, which are also used as examples and illustrations throughout the book.

Taken together, Table 2.1 and Figure 2.1 give some indication of what this means, when we move beyond ventures based upon only science and technology and active in high-tech sectors. Most existing studies in related areas focus on high-tech industries.

The AEGIS project and related literature also demonstrate that knowledge matters in a variety of different settings, including high-tech, low-tech and services alike. We find that it is possible to categorize the dimensions and indicators within these three broad categories of sectors, as shown in Table 2.1.

Table 2.1   How knowledge and innovation matters in low-tech, high-tech and service sectors

Low-tech	High-tech	Services
• Innovativeness of organization • Application of science-based activities and technologies in these low-tech sectors • Complex practical knowledge, such as operational knowledge • Potential for high growth products and services in what are often low growth sectors	• Innovativeness of product • Innovativeness of the technology • Dynamics of knowledge intensive sectors • R&D based • Science based • Academic education	• Innovativeness of business model • Innovation in the public sector • Academic education (some cases) • Design and creative industries

Table 2.1 tells us that we need to consider what concepts like 'knowledge intensity', 'innovativeness' or 'growth potential' really mean in these three different types of sectors. Services rely upon one mode of delivery and value creation as compared to manufacturing, for example. Each concept in Table 2.1 can also be turned into indicators, or data, about these phenomena. This is an interesting task to undertake. There are many different possible statistical indicators and ways of measuring the knowledge intensity in different types of sectors, as well as understanding the relative 'innovativeness' of product and services.

We can also think of the content of what is included or excluded as follows, based upon Malerba and McKelvey (2010).

Regardless of the specific sector, the KIE ventures are involved in entrepreneurship in the broad sense of systemic, problem-solving processes; embedded in innovation systems; affected by their institutional context; and open to innovative opportunities (Malerba and McKelvey, 2010).

Another way that they are presented and is relevant to think about is that a KIE venture should have the following four characteristics:

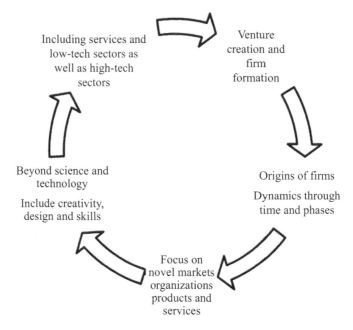

Figure 2.1   Focusing beyond R&D

1.   new firms
2.   innovative
3.   significant knowledge intensity
4.   exploit innovative opportunities in many sectors.

Innovative opportunities are discussed in more detail below, but mean that the firms have the possibility to sell their products and services, often in newly created markets. These innovative opportunities can be created through linking scientific, technological or creative knowledge with market needs and applications; using factors internal to the firm and external in the development of the venture; accessing key knowledge and resources through networks.

Accordingly, following Malerba and McKelvey (2010), we can elaborate as follows.

The KIE definition focuses on new firms, and by doing so, we exclude existing firms (over eight years old), innovation in existing firms and corporate entrepreneurship. By focusing upon innovative firms, we mean firms that translate knowledge into novel goods and services for sale. Therefore, we exclude those which focus upon standard (or well-established) goods and services, without elements of novelty in the product, process, organization, service and so on. By focusing on significant knowledge intensity, we exclude certain types of knowledge. We exclude repetitive and routine as well as well-known and established science and technology – that is, if these knowledge elements do not also contain elements of novel applications and modifications. By focusing upon innovative opportunities, we are particularly interested in firms involved in market activities, and therefore we have excluded NGOs, lifestyle firms (if not tied to a firm) and ones without any profit motive at all.

This book primarily focuses on KIE as a business proposition, that is, business start-ups and venture creation in the private sector, and these businesses have the above four specific characteristics. Thus, the book primarily discusses the processes of engaging, learning and evaluating at the level of KIE ventures.

We realize that we are excluding other types of entrepreneurship, such as starting a hairdresser. Many other types of entrepreneurship, start-up companies and small- and medium-sized enterprises (SMEs) also exist but are not the focus here. Our analysis will also end up excluding some variables that may be very important for these other types such as necessity, lifestyle or social entrepreneurship.

Moreover, there are some issues with the boundaries to innovation processes in general, and who will come up with new ideas to solve grand societal challenges. Indeed, large firms, NGOs, governments and so on will contribute to – and help coordinate – the complex processes required in order to provide new solutions to make society better. They are sometimes referred to in this book, especially due to the overlap with innovations. In the special cases of companies, this is when existing companies start up corporate spin-offs and develop new organizational forms for innovation. For government, the special case is the impact of public policy.

Our analysis suggests that three differentiating characteristics of KIE ventures should be understood. They are focus on:

1. specific role of different types of knowledge in entrepreneurship
2. interactions between individual and business ventures with the ecosystem and external environment
3. design thinking in the creation of opportunities and the creative process of entrepreneurship.

We shall explore in terms of (1) the specific role of different types of knowledge in entreprencurship, and what it means that KIE ventures are specific types of firms reliant upon different types of advanced, systematic knowledge. This does not have to come from universities and basic science. This knowledge that helps the business ventures compete may come from many sources, such as from design to science but it must be translated and changed to fit customer wants and market needs.

We shall discuss in terms of (2) the interactions between individual and business ventures with the ecosystem and external environment, and what this means for starting, managing and measuring performance of KIE ventures. There may be opportunities created through markets, technologies and institutions. This impact from the external environment may take the form of resources used in the initial phase, but also the role of external actors and phenomena in shaping the KIE venture. Research suggests that the KIE venture's choices in relation to internal management processes and accessing external knowledge and resources are partly dependent upon the external environment.

In terms of (3), the focus on design thinking in the creation of opportunities and the creative process of entrepreneurship, the book explains the thinking and proposes tools and techniques to enable better decision-making. This also means that while the decisions and strategies of individual and entrepreneurial ventures will impact performance, so will the changes and realignment to elements in the environment such as networks, relationship to customers and understanding of science.

These three characteristics taken together lead to our perspective on KIE. Entrepreneurship is often taught and studied as an activity pursued by a specific type of individual, called an entrepreneur, who starts a new company or business venture. There are also many hands-on books for writing business plans, which provide useful knowledge about how to start a business.[1] But the basic argument in this book differs in order to strive to understand the complexity as represented in these statements but also to structure clear phases and variables to help decision-making. The next sections explain each of these three differentiating characteristics in turn.

2.3   KNOWLEDGE AND KNOWLEDGE INTENSITY

This book focuses only upon KIE and not other types of entrepreneurship. The reason is that we see it as a nexus for explaining phases in the development of firms over time, and for explaining how different types of knowledge are translated into business performance. Another way of putting the main point is: KIE is a useful focusing device in order to discuss how societal organizations (like firms) can translate ideas and opportunities through their internal organization and their external networks into profits and new products and services.

The literature suggests that knowledge is distinct from data and information. Data are described as having no meaning, a series of inputs, providing the raw material from which information is produced. Information is the next level and is defined as data that has been organized into patterns enabling the extrapolation of meaning (Antonelli, 1999). Cook and Brown (1999) take the concept of knowledge a step further by differentiating between knowledge and knowing. They suggest that knowledge is about possession while knowing is about interaction between the knower and the world. This distinction assists the present research by providing increasing depth to the research questions posed.

Hence, information acquisition refers to the capability to identify and acquire information. Effort in information acquisition routines mainly has three attributes: intensity, speed and direction (Zahra and George, 2002). The intensity and speed of a firm's attempts to identify and collect relevant information can determine the quality of a firm's acquisition capabilities. These activities vary in their richness and complexity, highlighting a need to have different areas of expertise within a firm to successfully internalize knowledge from externally generated information (Rocha, 1997).

Knowledge utilization is equally emphasized as an important factor in innovation activities (von Hippel, 1988; Cockburn and Henderson, 1998; Chesbrough, 2003). For example, according to Chesbrough (2003), openness to using external sources of information and ideas in the firm's innovation processes, as well as interaction among different partners is of high importance when creating value through innovation activities. Knowledge utilization refers to assimilation, transformation and exploitation of new knowledge (Zahra and George, 2002), and hence covers the routines and processes that allow the entrepreneur to analyse, process, interpret and understand the information obtained from external sources, as well as the actual implementation of new knowledge.

Concerning these types of processes and phenomena, it is particularly interesting to consider knowledge as it plays a role in the initiation, development and output of innovative opportunities. The firm must both acquire appropriate information and utilize the knowledge within the firm. So let us very shortly focus on what is knowledge, and why this is such a significant variable that we can define a specific type of entrepreneurship as being knowledge intensive. Let us illustrate the importance of different types of knowledge. Entrepreneurial start-ups rely on three major types of knowledge: market, scientific and technological, and business.

A first type of relevant knowledge involves scientific, technological and creative knowledge. This type of knowledge is generally learned as the result of many years of study, and so the experts here are often natural scientists and engineers as well as creative artists and design specialists. They like to develop clever things and apply their expertise to solve problems and offer solutions. Most technical experts work in private companies, and so they work under cost constraints. They are taught to design to technical specifications and specific project deliverables. These natural scientists and engineers could still often imagine better scientific and technical solutions to company and societal problems. They could do so – if someone would just give them the necessary time and budget to solve things. The creative artists and design specialists could work in private companies or the public sector or as freelancers, and their focus is upon the creative process and artistic expressions.

Market knowledge refers to information gathered from past and current customers and the market – but also to an idea of what future buyers may want. Since we are talking about KIE as a business proposition, someone or some organization must be willing to buy the product, licence or service at sale for a price. This is sometimes called a 'business model', in relating what the firm makes or does to what the customers want. If the customers or buyers don't buy, then something is incorrect in what the KIE ventures thought they knew about market knowledge. Many things could be wrong, including their overall interpretation of the market as many actors buy and sell similar things. The price may be too high (or more occasionally, too low in the case of some services like consultancy where high price may be thought to signal high quality). The customers may want different technologies or performance attributes. The competitors may be offering something that is better, cheaper or more useful for other reasons. Hence, market knowledge includes understanding what customers want or are willing to buy, but also an understanding of the market dynamics and industrial dynamics over time.

The third main type of knowledge is business knowledge. Business knowledge has to do with running the company, both internally and externally. Internally involves things like running the company through organizational design and management techniques and externally through things like networks, relating to government regulations and so on. Much of this type of knowledge cannot be codified as laws and principles in the way that scientific and technological can be codified and taught. Business knowledge has to do with facing uncertainty and risk, trying reasonably right solutions and finding new paths forward. Hence, this business knowledge has to do with both 'knowing' and 'doing' business.

These three domains of knowledge – market, scientific, technological and creative, and internal to the firm business – are key to all firms but especially to KIE ventures. Entrepreneurs working in this way can be seen as 'knowledge operators' who work at the intersection between science, technology, creative industries, innovation and markets. Stimulating activity in this intersection between different types of knowledge should therefore be the primary result of public policy. Moreover, the ones involved may utilize existing knowledge, because they combine different knowledge assets or they create new types of knowledge. There are very different ways of measuring each type of knowledge, and quantitative studies and qualitative studies do not always indicate similar results.

2.4 KIE VENTURES AS INTERACTIONS FOR OPPORTUNITIES

A major question is how and why opportunities arise, outside the venture per se or perhaps more correctly, in interactions between the individual entrepreneur or venture, on the one hand, and the ecosystem and external environment, on the other.[2] Three main answers have been given in the literature – market, technological and internal business – which mirror the three major types of knowledge introduced above.

Generally speaking, within the entrepreneurship literature, a dominant line of thought is 'entrepreneurial opportunities'. The main idea is that market imperfections create the possibility for the entrepreneur to capture price differentials and thereby introduce non-equilibrium as an emergent property of the economy (Carlsson et al., 2012). The idea of 'entrepreneurial opportunities' can be traced back to the Austrian school of economics (Hayek, 1945). According to this perspective, the role of the entrepreneur is to observe market imperfections, and to eliminate differences in prices through introducing products and services. The entrepreneur exploits market imperfections due to the possibility of gaining arbitrage profits (Kirzner, 1973, 1982). This type of view of entrepreneurial opportunities has led to a certain emphasis in the literature upon the specific and idiosyncratic patterns of opportunity identification and pursuit. Ardichvili et al. (2003) argue that the individual entrepreneur is more or less able to identify these market opportunities and develop a venture based upon: (1) entrepreneurial alertness; (2) information asymmetries and prior (individual) knowledge; (3) social networks; (4) personality traits; and (5) the type of opportunity. Hence, the main structural explanation for entrepreneurial opportunities can be seen to be the 'market', especially how market imperfections enable arbitrage profits. However, given that these market imperfections could theoretically be visible to all entrepreneurs, much of the literature stressing this type of opportunity tends to try to find explanations at the level of characteristics and traits of the individual entrepreneur. This has also led to a central discussion in entrepreneurship research about the origin of opportunities (Shane and Venkataraman, 2000; Eckhardt and Shane, 2003; Sarason et al., 2006; Vaghely and Julien, 2010).

An important concept within evolutionary and Schumpeterian economics has been 'technological opportunities'. This has been seen as a key concept of how science and technological knowledge help drive economic development. Scherer (1965) put forth the argument that technological opportunities help explain the differential propensity of firms in different sectors to patent and innovate. He argued that 'differences in technological opportunity – e.g. differences in technical investment possibilities unrelated to the mere volume of sales and typically opened up by the broad advance of knowledge – are a major factor responsible for inter-industry differences in inventive output' (Scherer, 1965, p. 1121). This type of literature often tries to explain major differences amongst industries, and the role of technological knowledge in stimulating growth. Breschi et al. (2000, pp. 390–1) argue that 'observed sectoral patterns of innovative activities are related to the nature of the relevant technological regimes ... defined by the specific combination of technological opportunities, appropriability of innovations, cumulativeness of technical advance and the properties of the knowledge base underlying firms' innovative activities'. This concept thus places the firms' own investment into R&D activities into an idea that their probability of finding an invention and later innovation is dependent not only on the firm per se, but the likelihood of discovering new knowledge and the overall rate of change in this type of knowledge. The firm's willingness to invest in R&D and innovation are often explicitly tied to a discussion of appropriability, that is, about whether the firm will secure the rewards for themselves. In contrast, when knowledge is not appropriated, it can have spill-over effects upon competitors.

Rather than 'technological opportunities', we would like to see a broader category of 'scientific, technological and creative opportunities', which reflects the particular role of a wide variety of human creativity in coming up with solutions to interesting problems and providing new and unexpected products and services. This would allow us to consider not only the scientific and technological knowledge inside and outside the firm, but especially whether and how the firm can make use of scientific, technological and creative knowledge in different ways inside the firm.

This also matters in understanding the role of such knowledge inside the firm, that is, how these types of knowledge are used in the internal business model to appropriate value for the venture.

The concept of 'productive opportunities' is used within theories of the firm from a resource-based and knowledge-based perspective. This refers more to the internal firm organization of resources and competencies, but the value of reconfiguring those resources is to better succeed in the market. Penrose (1959), who is often seen as the pioneer in these theories, stressed that opportunities are not market perfection, but arise from the possibilities to combine the internal resources of a firm in various ways. How those resources are deployed will affect the firm's growth and profitability, but these are limited by the managers' capacity to envision alternative modes. More modern literature, like Hamel and Prahalad (1989), take into account factors that are internal and external to the firm through the concept of strategic intent, whereby the internal resource base should not limit growth possibilities. Teece et al. (1997) stress that firms can develop dynamic capabilities, consisting of positions, paths and processes. They argue that the possibility to reconfigure the firm is limited by the firm's historical development in terms of paths that it has followed over time, and by the organizational and managerial processes used to leverage existing resources and access new ones. Moreover, KIE ventures tend to be young and small, so that their view of productive opportunities has to focus upon how they can combine their access to resources and ideas in the external environment with internal management and development processes.

Thus, by taking into account these two levels – of venture creation as a management process and as a broader phenomenon – also enables us to discuss the relationships between the decision-making for the company in relation to the broader business and societal context. The venture can access resource and realize opportunities through a series of decisions, which lead to the balancing of alternative logics between business planning and emergence of unexpected opportunities.

The concept of 'innovative opportunities' was explicitly developed to address the strengths and shortcoming of these existing discussions of opportunities (Holmèn et al., 2007). What does in fact constitute an opportunity, and how are opportunities related to KIE ventures? Holmén et al. (2007) develop the argument that 'innovative opportunities' actually arise from the systemic interaction between the three types of opportunities and provide details of the process.

This argument is of particular relevance to the concept of these phenomena, as the fundamental reasoning is that it could arise in both high-tech, low-tech and service industries, that it may stem from individual as well as team actions and that it may create a diverse range of effects. Hence, following Holmén et al. (2007), we argue that an innovative opportunity for KIE consists of at least the following three conceptual elements in order for actors to have the opportunity to identify, act upon and realize the potential inherent in an idea:

- an economic value for someone
- a possibility that the resources needed to realize the opportunity can be mobilized
- a possibility that at least some part of the generated economic value can be appropriated by the actor pursuing the opportunity.

The question then is how the entrepreneur can realize the economic value, opportunity and generated economic value in specific situations. This leads us to the concepts of created and designed opportunities.

2.5 INNOVATIVE OPPORTUNITIES AS CREATED AND DESIGNED

How are innovative opportunities created and designed when we take a dynamic process view? Chapter 6 addresses this literature in detail, so the purpose here is to give a simple introduction to design thinking.

For this book, what is important about design thinking when conceptualizing a KIE venture is to position this clearly in relation to the concept of opportunities, emphasizing questions such as: How are opportunities created/perceived? Who and what is involved in opportunities? How are opportunities exploited? And with what effect? We see that the concept of innovative opportunities resulting from an emerging design process also differentiates our way of thinking from other ways of conceptualizing entrepreneurial opportunities.

Our view is that design thinking plays an important role in the successful exploration and exploitation of KIE. From our perspective, the opportunities for KIE ventures and these processes and phenomena can be seen as resulting from an emerging design process. By design we mean how aspiring entrepreneurs deliberately engage in the creative design of a new entrepreneurial opportunity (Van de Ven et al., 1984; Casson and Nisar, 2007; Nielsen et al., 2012). This literature provides us with much insight into how these processes and phenomena can be achieved through the application of design as creative processes to generate something better or different compared to what already exists, and as an action aimed at transforming the present into a preferred and more desirable future situation (Orlikowski, 2004).

Chapter 6 argues that applying design thinking to KIE could be a powerful way of framing opportunities and of understanding the phenomena. This is because there is always a combination between the rational planning and knowing of variables that are important along with the doing and messy empirical reality. Design thinking provides us with a strong foundation for thinking about KIE as a process of design of innovative opportunities. By this we mean it reflects the overall dynamic interplay between phases and variables, illustrating how the understanding of innovative opportunities are being derived from technological, entrepreneurial and productive opportunities, and the notion that opportunities may be actively designed in a process of combining both creation and discovery of opportunities.

2.6 FROM A LINEAR PROCESS TO AN INTERACTIVE MODEL

Our KIE creation model is an interactive model, which takes into consideration the three special characteristics discussed above. But how can we think about processes and causality in relation to complex topics like the role of different types of knowledge in entrepreneurship, the interactions between individual and business ventures with the ecosystem and external environment and how innovative opportunities are designed.

As with many processes, when thinking about entrepreneurship, the easiest way to approach the phenomena is to start by thinking of a linear process. A linear model suggests direction and starts with inputs, then moves to a development process, which leads to outputs. This is illustrated in Figure 2.2.

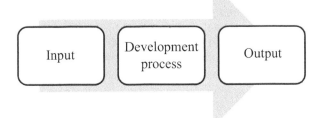

Figure 2.2   From input through development process to output

The linear view is useful, and indeed, this book talks about business phases that roughly correspond to these three. Indeed, many approaches in starting a venture or in influencing job creation through public policy tend to use this type of linear approach for analysis.

One advantage is that the process is easy to communicate. There are three phases, and the direction of causality runs in one direction. One can decide where there are problems, analyse them and have the impression that the overall process is easy to manage. You access financing and can start a new Google. You encourage university researchers to start companies by giving them soft loans, and you have created a new industry.

Another advantage of the linear process view is that it facilitates business planning. Planning provides a way of deciding what is needed and in setting targets for each phase. Planning in a simple sense also makes it seem like the starting of a company is easy, in that you decide what you need to access in terms of ideas and resources, and just do it. Planning helps define answers to questions about 'who, what, where and why' and helps focus attention on the need to take decisions.

There are also advantages in evaluation. The venture capitalist as well as the public policy organization invest in inputs or support the development process, and they need measurements and want to know that their resources and ideas have impact. They want to be able to evaluate especially whether the inputs invested lead to a good outcome in terms of reasonable and measurable outputs. Many examples exist on how evaluation is done, such as when the venture capitalist manages to take a venture to an initial public offering (IPO) or when the public policy agency claims they helped start ten new companies from a joint research centre.

But the real world is more complex. Deciding upon the targets is not necessarily the same thing as reaching those targets. Deciding what to evaluate as an outcome of this type of public policy is usually more complex than counting firms or patents. The outputs that are easily or commonly measured do not always correspond to the most interesting impacts of entrepreneurship.

Our KIE creation model balances simplicity with more complex feedback loops. Our model consists of three phases, and also second-order variables that are key in succeeding with entrepreneurship, as seen in Figure 2.3.

This figure provides a visualization. It is built upon both an understanding of the key phases and relevant second-order variables as well as the complexities noted above in the special characteristics of KIE.

The model is still simplistic and allows for an understanding of directionality and change over time, which is the essence of a linear

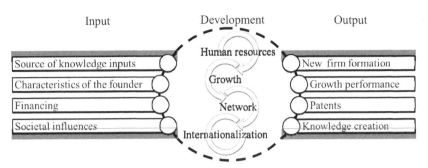

Figure 2.3   The KIE creation model

model. Indeed, even the visualization demonstrates that our KIE model is somewhat related to the linear process model presented above. Both convey a sense of change and development over time, what these dynamics represent is an important aspect of understanding the phenomena of entrepreneurship. This is useful for comprehension.

We simultaneously try to balance that simplicity with more complex feedback loops, for example, that the phase of managing and developing the venture may require changes to the resources and ideas accessed or that characteristics and traits of founders may later impact performance. Linear models are good for remembering the basic issues. However, if you want to influence things, then you need to go beyond a simple linear process view to more complex, dynamic systems with feedback loops. This is particularly true in all processes involving human beings, with their complex individual traits and organizational forms.

Therefore, our KIE creation model highlights three main phases, but with different wording to reflect the propositions and underlying understanding of the phenomena. Instead of inputs, we shall discuss accessing resources and ideas, as these are the key elements of the creation of venture and business founding phase. Thus, rather than the development phase, we focus upon managing and developing the KIE venture, and instead of outputs, we call it evaluating performance and outputs in deciding what and how to evaluate, which requires a good evaluation design. These are also the titles of Chapters 3, 4 and 5, so the purpose in this chapter is a very short introduction to the overall model.

These three overall phases reflect an understanding of KIE ventures as being designed through a complex process of interacting variables, internally and externally. This view also links directly to the second proposition of this book, about the need to balance. During the exploration, creation and exploitation of entrepreneurship we see, on the one hand, the complexity and multitude of variables and, on the other hand, our striving for a model limited to the key phases and variables. Thus, the reader can use what they have learned about the model to help engage in, and evaluate, the performance and outputs. It is in this way that an evidence-based approach helps find knowledge, which is applicable and useful in practical situations.

These phases and their second-order variables naturally mirror debates in the existing literature within entrepreneurship in general, given a long debate in recent years as regards to how and why certain inputs affect firm formation and performance. Each variable reflects a broad topic in its own right in the general entrepreneurship literature. However, when discussing this type of entrepreneurship, the systematic literature review shows that these are the key variables, which often play a specific role in relation to the management of KIE ventures and the stimulation of entrepreneurship. We acknowledge that this also means that certain variables are excluded here, if they are of more marginal importance,

2.7 PHASES AND KEY VARIABLES IN THE MODEL

KIE has been introduced as processes and phenomena, one where knowledge plays a particularly important role in the generation of ideas and their utilization into innovations, and one where management and development entail a process of design of innovative opportunities. This section deals with the three phases in more detail, including the second-order variables. These are the important ones that need to be taken into consideration in order to create a frame for understanding the management of KIE ventures and the stimulation of this type of entrepreneurship.

2.7.1 Accessing Resources and Ideas: Inputs

The first phase we consider in the conceptual framework of KIE addresses accessing resources and ideas: inputs to KIE ventures. With this phase of venture creation and business founding, we refer to what can be called prerequisites and antecedents. Existing structures in the ecosystem affect the formation of this type of new venture. From the KIE venture perspective, this is not only about inputs. The phase is about accessing because the challenge is how to access resources and ideas, as well as understanding how and why previous network relationships and the ability to access things externally will influence the firm's later development.

By definition, this phase precedes the creation of a venture or founding of the firm, and hence all variables are 'outside' the firm initially but are later moved in, or accessed externally and translated internally into relevant business models. It is important to think through which types of knowledge resources are accessed, how the entrepreneur and founding team are linked to the ecosystem as these will affect phases. Four related variables, in particular, will impact how innovative opportunities are created and designed between the KIE venture and external environment and are included in the KIE model as particularly crucial (Figure 2.4):

- sources of knowledge inputs
- characteristics and traits of founders
- financing
- societal influences and public policy.

One crucial input relates to the sources of knowledge inputs. This literature identifies a variety of sources from which KIE ventures arise or take resources, for example, if they are spin-offs from corporate firms or from universities, and whether the entrepreneur is experienced or *de novo* entrant. These sources have been shown to impact the development and success of the new venture.

Generally speaking, studying the characteristics or traits of entre-preneurs (founders) is very prevalent in the field, and this is also reflected in the research related to KIE. Here the study of the characteristics of the individual focuses on specific traits related to the knowledge intensive entrepreneur, for example, cognitive and behavioural studies on the way knowledge intensive entrepreneurs differ from 'regular' entrepreneurs as well as the intentions and motivations behind starting a new venture.

Financing entrepreneurship is also a topic that receives much attention in the fields of finance and entrepreneurship as well as in research addressing policy issues and often in regard to venture capital and in relation to the common metaphor 'death valley', where no financing is available in certain phases. Financing issues refer to, for example, different types of risk finance, their effect on the venture, and so on. Here, we concentrate on what types exist and how they influence the KIE venture.

Societal influences address issues such as incubators and science parks, which focus upon how society and public policy can stimulate developments. Many of these are applied for regional development. Questions we should ask about the purpose of public policy in order to understand their impact on the development of KIE are: Do we want

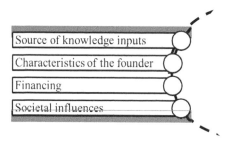

Figure 2.4   Input to KIE creation

entrepreneurs, regardless of type and industry? Or should public policy stimulate specific types of entrepreneurs?

Chapter 3, 'Accessing resources and ideas:' explains the impacts of these variables upon the KIE venture and on this type of entrepreneurship.

2.7.2   Managing and Developing KIE Ventures

The second phase concerns managing and developing the KIE venture. This phase refers to the processes of managing and developing internally and externally to the company. This is largely an internal process, referring to the internal competences, resources and approaches affecting the management and growth of the new venture after initial formation. However, many of these variables require interacting with the external environment, but the combination of knowledge and internal and external processes and organizations is what results in the design of opportunities and their realization through business models (Figure 2.5).

The first variable addresses the topic of human resources. This topic is popular and addressed in the management literature at large, but is an issue of great interest to entrepreneurship, due to its direct correlation to growth and survival. Human resources issues cover a range of different aspects related to entrepreneurship, such as, for example, types of personnel hired in KIE, problems related to the availability of knowledge employees, impact of prior experience of employees, challenges related to the varying roles of owner/founder/manager and incentive schemes.

The second variable deals with aspects of networks, which includes related topics like social capital. Literature on social capital and networks shows that these are important concepts in order to understand the entrepreneurial process and how the social networking affects knowledge

Figure 2.5   Development of KIE ventures

intensive firms' performance. Social capital is an important concept in this stream of literature. The exact definition varies somewhat but usually emphasizes the relational aspect – meaning, for example, that it is produced in social interaction (for example, Anderson et al., 2007). Relational capability (Capaldo, 2007) is the firm's capability to gain competitive advantage by creating and managing its network of social relations. Other similar concepts, related to social capital and often used in the literature, are social networks, strategic linkages and alliances. They relate to social aspects, and also include aspects like entrepreneurial teams, the formal and informal relationships the KIE venture has with different types of networks (academia, industry, investors or customers), what such network relationships are used for and at which stages, collaborative intellectual property rights (IPR) and so on.

The third variable has to do with growth patterns, and can be considered in relation to the process of developing KIE ventures and the tensions that arise. One of the topics often highlighted in both the entrepreneurship and innovation management literature is related to the difficulties experienced by many firms in creating balance between R&D activities and activities focusing on bringing products efficiently to market. Going back to a classical distinction introduced by March (1991), this phenomenon can generally be seen as the 'exploration' versus 'exploitation' trade-off. However, for KIE ventures, the literature suggests there are very specific and particular difficulties in balancing R&D and market foci.

The final variable discussed for managing and developing KIE ventures is internationalization. Internationalization is of particular interest to KIE ventures, given that the knowledge and innovative opportunities created often have global potential, and they are not restricted to regional or national boundaries. In an international knowledge economy, KIE serves as a key mechanism for societies and economies, by which knowledge created in one organization becomes commercialized in a new venture, and likewise, how knowledge created in one country is developed or applied in another.

2.7.3 Evaluating Performance and Outputs

The third and final overall phase is related to evaluating performance and outputs. This discussion concerns the different types of outcome generated through KIE and, more broadly, the effects of this output on economic growth and social well-being as well as how to measure performance and outputs.

This phase can be discussed either at the level of the KIE venture, at which point we mean inside the firm, or at the level of KIE, which is more related to impacts on public policy and society.

This topic is indeed of great interest as the fundamental interest in KIE is based on the understanding that KIE creates positive and above-average output. When public policy is focused upon KIE, it is generally because there is a view or belief in the ability of KIE to stimulate economic growth and development (Figure 2.6).

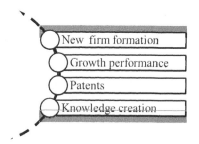

Figure 2.6   Output and performance of KIE

The first measure addresses the amount and impact of new firms in different industries and academic disciplines. The proxy of number of new firms is often used as the main measure and indicator of entre-preneurial activity at the policy level. The impact created by new firm formation is potentially a more interesting measure, yet more rarely used, due to difficulties of finding reliable statistics on impact.

The second measure is the actual performance of the KIE venture created through growth. Measuring the performance of new ventures is of interest because they are a major source of job creation and improvement in performance is critical to their survival and growth. However, collecting data on the performance of new ventures is often difficult due to a lack of historical information and accessibility. There are also major differences in what is defined as growth, including a variety of proxy measures such as sales, employees, venture capital obtained and so on. A related measure is the number of new firms generated in different industries or academic areas.

The third topic identified as a way to evaluate performance and output is patenting and IPR. Patenting is a proxy used for measuring the output of innovation and entrepreneurship alike, but the appropriateness of this measure has continuously been a source of debate. Naturally, there is literature on how patenting from different types of KIE occurs as well as topics like the use of patents in relation to firm strategy and the importance of patents for future activities, among others.

Finally, an increasing focus has also been given to knowledge creation as a measure for output of KIE. Knowledge in this context is considered and measured in terms of cluster formation stemming from certain knowledge domains, increases in the academic focus on certain technology, the increased knowledge domain of the individual KIE venture in terms of numbers of highly educated employees and so on.

2.8 SUMMARY

This chapter has explained what we mean by the propositions that KIE is a special form of venture creation. We have described KIE phenomena as a series of decisions that must balance between business planning and the emergence of unexpected opportunities. The reader should better understand the two ideas, or propositions that this chapter has discussed:

- *KIE is a special form of venture creation and different from other types of entrepreneurship. The key focus here is in the relationships between KIE venture creation and business phases and context.*
- *KIE is achieved through a series of decisions that lead to the creation of balance between business planning and the emergence of unexpected opportunities. A number of structures and variables are identifiable and must be considered when planning the development of a new company. But the interpretation of such variables may result in a variety of different outcomes.*

The discussions on definitions and the interrelating concepts of knowledge, opportunities and design thinking lead us to the KIE creation model.

Three elements have been described that position our perspective and the type of entrepreneurship compared with general entrepreneurship literature. They are the focus on the (1) specific role of different types of knowledge in entrepreneurship; (2) the interactions between individual and business ventures with the ecosystem and external context; and (3) the focus on opportunities created and designed through these interactions with the ecosystem.

Our purpose here is therefore different from the one-off entrepreneurial experience. It is to use an evidence-based approach to develop the conceptual framework, which is visualized in our model. Visualizations, together with the underlying conceptual framework, help to structure our understanding of the action of engaging in entrepreneurship, as well as the steps involved in the process of founding and managing a KIE venture. This chapter therefore provides a KIE creation model including three phases and second-order variables.

Understanding the KIE creation model and phenomena should enable the reader to use them as a knowledge platform for learning about, engaging in and evaluating performance. This evidence-based approach thus draws upon a systematic literature review that was a starting point, which was then further developed into our model of KIE.

The actual experience of starting a firm often involves a chaotic process, with multiple and simultaneous decisions having to be taken. So, though a structure of understanding, this model can be used to help navigate critical events and decision-points, as they occur along a process of venture creation and management.

One contribution of this book is that the reader can therefore relate the KIE creation model and conceptual framework to decision-making. This should help position the learning – or used in the creation and development of a specific venture – to understand what to do, relative to the more general case. For example, it can be helpful to specify whether key elements are missing, whether opportunities are being missed or whether network partners may be used to obtain key complementary assets. The model helps frame what we 'know' about KIE, and can be applied to individual learning processes when starting a firm.

The following chapters are structured around this exact frame of understanding, initiated through input, developed through management processes and evaluated through measures of performance and output.

NOTES

1. Of course, many courses and books exist on making a business plan, or how to make a 30-second elevator pitch to a venture capitalist or how to report business data in relation to national regulations. These are all important elements, which are widely available elsewhere but not included in this book. Still, this book is useful in 'doing' and 'engaging' in entrepreneurship in a different way.
2. This section draws heavily from previous work between Maureen McKelvey and the co-authors Magnus Holmèn and Mats Magnusson.

3. Accessing resources and ideas

3.1 INTRODUCTION

This chapter focuses upon accessing resources and ideas. These can be seen as inputs affecting KIE and venture creation. There are some aspects that are directly related to the individual founder, and some related to how to access resources and ideas from the external environment.

This chapter addresses the processes and KIE phenomena before the venture is created. The proposition for this chapter is as follows:

Accessing inputs, which are resources and ideas, is crucial to starting the company. This phase refers to the processes and phenomena before the venture is created, but also takes up subjects like financing that remain relevant during later management phases. The emphasis is on how and why to use resources and ideas that are linked to the founder or that can be transferred from the ecosystem and external environment to the venture. This focus on inputs reflects the fact that KIE ventures rarely come out of the blue. Indeed, the KIE venture often draws upon existing organizations, and this leads to many decisions about how and why to use them to balance planning and emergent opportunities.

So, even though we talk about resources and ideas as inputs, this does not mean that they only exist before the venture is created, or pre-venture. Indeed, KIE ventures must continually access some variables, especially financing, in order to support their opportunity recognition and real-ization. Thus, in that sense, KIE ventures must continue to create and design their opportunities. They need knowledge from the domains of the scientific, the technological and the creative; from the market; and from business. These types of knowledge often require different mindsets, and the founder must combine them in some ways in order to design an organization that can recognize and realize the opportunities and turn them into the business. Combining knowledge also involves the inter-action between opportunities, internal processes and the external environ-ment and ecosystem. This also means that some dimensions during this phase will be under direct managerial control, whereas other dimensions can be used but only by accessing them externally, such as through networks and social capital. This chapter addresses four main types of resources and ideas, as illustrated in Figure 3.1.

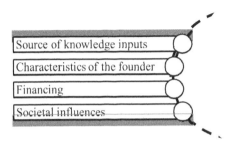

Figure 3.1   Input to KIE creation

Section 3.2 discusses the sources of knowledge, inputs that focus upon resources and ideas that the founder brings into the firm, through previous experience, skills and networks with people, firms and others. These sources help the venture in accessing resources and ideas, particularly through the different types of knowledge available and channelled into the KIE venture. The networks may be valuable for any of the different types of knowledge needed.

A key issue in the literature on KIE ventures has in recent years been on identifying from where the venture emerges, for example, from a parent organization. This leads to classifications about spin-offs from either academia or companies and about the degree to which these processes are 'planned' or 'just happen'. The most relevant pre-history for KIE ventures of the sources of knowledge are usually considered university spin-offs and corporate spin-offs. However, there are also many independent entrepreneurs, who either have few or informal ties to others, given that resources may move out of firms and organizational forms and into new ventures without explicit approval or longer term relationships.

Section 3.3 discusses the characteristics and traits of the entrepreneur and founder, irrespective of whether we refer to the individual or the team. Fields like sociology and cognitive science have focused upon many issues related to what makes some individuals more likely to accept the risk and uncertainty involved in choosing this career path. Moreover, in recent decades, the debate on opportunity recognition and mobilization has been in strong focus, and links the cognitive dimension to the learning dimensions, such as previous employment history and experimental learning. The most relevant aspects for KIE ventures are the characteristics that relate the founders to how they access resources and ideas or influence later firm performance.

Section 3.4 looks at financing, which is known to be a very important variable and to influence general entrepreneurship. KIE ventures need to find capital, and to find lenders who are willing to take on the risk of investing in something which may have unproven technologies, unproven products and a lack of market knowledge. There are many different types of financing used. Although venture capital and IPOs receive much attention in the process of starting up technology companies in particular, there is alternative financing that is used, including smaller scale individual, family and private funding as well as larger scale corporate venture capital.

Section 3.5 addresses societal influences and public policy. These are broader ways of trying to stimulate KIE. Many of these public initiatives also provide financing and advice, in just the same way as venture capital and corporate venture capital does. This section primarily discusses incubators and the main benefits of geographical clustering, including the relationship to services.

3.2 SOURCES OF KNOWLEDGE INPUTS

For the knowledge intensive entrepreneur, the study of the sources of knowledge inputs is vital to designing business inputs and processes. This book has introduced three different types of knowledge: technological, scientific and creative; market; and business. What each is and how they are combined to form a particular set of products and services is generally difficult to define. There is an 'ambiguity' of knowledge, that is, that which may be valuable and used could vary in importance as the venture learns more about the demands and possibilities formulated by different types of stakeholders and networks. A technology may seem to be useful for one product, but turn out to actually find a market when, for example, it is incorporated into another product and completely different industry.

Business enterprises are involved in market transactions, per definition, but they are also involved in knowledge networks and other types of networks that influence their ability to identify opportunities and mobilize resources to commercialize ideas.

The most common sources of knowledge that are transferred initially into the KIE venture are those that are closely related to the founder. This section discusses the sources of knowledge resources and ideas, while the next one addresses the individual characteristics and traits. These individuals may be thought of as the persons who can identify potential opportunities based on their prior knowledge and experience of technology, market and industry. From this perspective, many insights and lessons can be drawn from the general entrepreneurship literature. The most relevant one is that KIE ventures probably do not appear from 'nowhere' but are instead related to organizations that specialize in knowledge creation such as universities, R&D labs and firms. Moreover, the value of these initial networks may decrease over time as the KIE venture starts to orientate towards other goals and develop new products and services.

This would imply that KIE ventures are not randomly distributed in terms of dynamic antecedents but instead their lineage can be traced to particular organizations that have highly educated people, focus upon the development of technological knowledge or creative industry, and application of that knowledge into innovations for the market. Another implication is that new ventures need to be analysed as a relationship between the individual firm within their context – such as innovation system, network or cluster – rather than as totally independent firms.

This section particularly focuses upon how knowledge such as resources, skilled people and competencies are transferred from a 'parent' organization to the new enterprise. In this way, the different sources of knowledge inputs to KIE are, at an aggregated level, highly related to the three different categories of KIE ventures introduced above, namely academic spin-offs, corporate spin-offs as well as independent start-ups founded by individuals with industrial experience.

KIE ventures can spin out from different organizational structures already existing, and so can also access resources and ideas from different organizations in society. This relates the discussion of knowledge inputs to the type of KIE venture.

- One type of venture comes from the large established company. This may lead to diversification within the company, or it may lead to new separate companies, known as corporate spin-offs. The parent company may or may not retain control over resources and ownership, and may or may not provide financing, what is known as corporate venture capital. Some of these spin-offs are 'planned and managed' while in many other cases, the employee simply leaves and starts a new venture.
- Another type of venture comes from universities, including academic researchers and students. This is usually assumed to be a

separate organizational structure, different from the university, known as an academic spin-off. The relationship to the parent organization may continue, however, in that the founding research-ers can remain as employees and students as students. Sometimes, the parent university does have control or partial ownership through initiatives such as entrepreneurial education programmes and tech-nology transfer offices.

- A third type discussed in the literature is called *de novo* entrants, or independent start-ups. Usually, one assumes that the entrepreneur is an individual, with a very small company and not coming from a related industry or large organization. The founders may be experi-enced or inexperienced. They are generally not seen as involving control, ownership or resource issues from a parent organization, as there are none.

- Finally, it is also likely that other types of parent organizations, less visible in KIE processes, may be very important to society. The parent organization may come from other organizational forms in society, such as public organizations stimulating start-ups, social entrepreneurship and community-based forms such as digital net-work or cooperatives. These are not discussed in this book, but may be useful to mention for future research foci.

The corporate spin-off and academic spin-off are discussed below, but with some comparison to the independent start-up. A key issue is whether the relationships are formal – such as continuing contracts and equity – or informal – such as the founder bringing industrial experience with him or her into the new venture.

Moreover, in relation to the KIE venture, the questions that we are interested in are: What are the impacts of different sources of knowledge on later venture performance? What are the relationships and comple-mentarities between the parent organization and the spin-off?

3.2.1 Corporate Spin-offs

Corporate venture capital is covered below in relation to financing, but what is worth introducing here is what happens when the venture is started by explicit actions of a large company. Corporate spin-offs are formal relationships whereas previously employees might just leave the larger existing company and start their own venture. For various reasons, companies have moved to more formal spin-offs and companies have tried to 'manage' these processes of spin-offs in recent years.

Therefore, in the case of corporate spin-offs, the source of the KIE is an established firm, which has identified a business opportunity that is deemed to lie outside the scope of the current business of the firm or when the firm decides to narrow down this scope to focus upon 'core competencies' and their main business.

A case where the large firm decides to no longer cover a product area and instead start up an independent organization can be illustrated by the following example of a medical technology firm.

> [The firm] decided to form a separate business area for the non-dental products. It was called Cranio-Facial Reconstruction and Audiology ('CFRA') ... In 1997 the top management decided that [the firm] should become 'a dentistry company' with two complementary businesses, viz., implants and prosthetics. The Chief Financial Officer therefore got the assignment to find a new environment for the CFRA business area. As preparation for sale a business plan for a conceivable new company was made. (Laage-Hellman, D 1.7.7. – Entific)

This illustration indicates that the large company played a major role in starting the KIE venture, and they tended to bring knowledge and experience from industries, about markets and about technologies to this new company.

Corporate spin-offs and managed processes are ways to help stimulate corporate spin-outs, rather than 'just letting it happen' when employees leave. Many large companies have had policies to stimulate corporate spin-offs, and these policies may or may not be linked to specific venture capital funds.

Examples of companies that at some time have had specific policies in this area include giants such as: 3M, British Gas Technology, British Telecom Cable & Wireless, Chevron, Ericsson, Intel, Procter & Gamble, SAAB AB, Siemens, Skandia, Telia, The Generics Group, The Technology Partnership Group and Unilever.

One can also study whether corporate spin-offs retain linkages to the new firms, or not, and whether those linkages are formal or informal. Parhankangas and Arenius (2003) studied 50 technology related spin-offs from large Finnish industrial firms. They proposed a taxonomy of corporate spin-off firms by exploring the nature of the relationship between parent firm and spin-off. Based on cluster analysis, the authors identified three distinct groups of corporate spin-off firms: spin-offs developing new technologies; spin-offs serving new markets; and restructuring spin-offs. Each group retains different types, and intensity, of relationships with the parent corporate organization. Thus, the degree of formality differs, usually, depending upon whether the start-up tries to compete with the parent organization or whether it competes instead in different industries or offers complementary products and services within one industry.

New venture founding over time is correlated with measures of the changing external entrepreneurial and business environment, suggesting that future research in this domain may need to more carefully examine such factors in the external environment.

3.2.2 University Spin-offs and Academic Spin-offs

Often, when the words 'KIE venture' are used, thoughts immediately turn to the university and topics like academic entrepreneurship and commercialization of science.

Thus, in the case of academic spin-offs, the source of KIE is naturally most often the research conducted at the university where the academic founders are or were employed prior to the KIE. In this way, academic spin-offs are mostly driven by the scientific and/or technical knowledge and experience of founders. The following case of a spin-off illustrates this point.

> The source of knowledge is the research environment at Aalborg University, Denmark ... the company GomSpace has commercialized the ideas that emerged during the research. The competencies acquired from the research are mainly technical. (AAU –1.2.4, GomSpace)

However, in a few cases, academic spin-offs are not founded by academic researchers but by recent graduate students.

> The firm was founded by two graduates (labelled 'Mr. X.' and 'Ms. Y.' below) of the University of Kassel, Germany, who had studied international agriculture there. Mr. X. wrote his thesis on quality issues in the drying process of fruits and vegetables, while Ms. Y. investigated the production of cocoa in South America. Both worked together on an internship in fruits drying in India and already decided there that starting a company in this business would be an option after graduating from the university. One of their professors (labelled Prof. Z. below) offered interested students to work on an experimental solar dryer. Ms. Y. and Mr. X. decided to sign up as volunteers ... The entrepreneurial process started in 2006. The founders were asked by the university in 2005 to represent their department at a regional event where they were supposed to sell experimentally produced dried fruits. Both were astonished how fast they sold 400 packages of dried cherries. The next day the local newspaper ran an article about the not-yet-existing firm and people started to phone the two students. After careful consideration they decided to give the idea a try. (MPI – d 1.3.x – CFGE2)

When relating to academic spin-offs, we generally think of researchers and professors as starting the companies, but in fact students also represent a strong driving force for commercializing science and technology.

Academic entrepreneurship may be defined to mean many things, but has primarily been analysed as the situation when university researchers and students commercialize science, specifically through patents and starting companies.

Academic spin-offs are new firms created to exploit commercial knowledge, such as technology or research results, that were developed within a university setting.

Indeed, much of the literature that can be used to understand KIE ventures is based on the subset that we can call university spin-offs. University spin-offs may be classified according to different criteria and measures. For example, they could be ones that are started either by researchers or students, and depending on who starts them one may be able to predict different things about the venture performance and societal impacts. Moreover, the university spin-offs may be classified in different industries, where technology and different types of knowledge are identified as the key asset in their business models.

Universities are the target of much public policy and of course represent one key area where advanced technical and scientific knowledge may be commercialized. Existing research suggests that these types of KIE ventures will have differential outcomes and they are highly impacted by the context.

Many existing studies on related terms like 'technology-based firms' are almost exclusively focused upon 'high-tech' industries. Even in low-tech industries, it is of course possible that there is a close tie to the university and linkages to scientific research, as this illustration shows.

> As for the second phase, [the firm] would go a step further and invest in research and development (R&D), with a strong emphasis in research. 'We want to be in the [technology] forefront. We know the [technology] state of the art... but we want [to develop new products] based on scientific research', says Mr. CC. This strategic (long term) goal allowed the entrepreneurial team to submit its business idea to the Technology Transfer Office of the local University and obtain the spin-off statute from this University. Three other factors were important to obtain the spin-off seal: Mr. PP was a former student of this University, the project was textile related which was relevant as the University has a strong Textile Engineering Department, and the business idea was innovative ... the University has been mostly a service provider (laboratory tests, industrial property and quality certification) of [the firm].' (UECE – d 1.3.X – CTP2)

Firm performance may also be impacted especially evaluating the impact of the founder in terms of having experience, education and specific technological competencies. These are all related to whether and what type of venture that will be created.

Pirnay et al. (2003) studied university spin-outs (USOs) and they discuss existing definitions of USOs in order to reconcile them and provide criteria for classifying and understanding the different facets of this concept. Their paper contributes by defining the boundaries of this concept and elucidating its variety through a typology. This relates directly to the characteristics and traits of the founder.

Their proposed typology is based on two key discriminatory factors, namely (1) the status of individuals involved in the new business venturing process (researchers or students) and (2) the nature of knowledge transferred from the university to the new venture (codified or tacit), which then leads to an understanding of the nature of the USO activities, namely whether they are product-oriented or service-oriented. Their paper can thus outline the different ways in which knowledge is diffused through individuals (for example, researchers or students) as well as the likely outcomes in terms of type of knowledge and final activities or products.

Another finding is whether university spin-offs are more or less likely to lead to growth and jobs in society. We use the example of one study from Sweden, Lindholm Dahlstrand (1997), the author of which studies new technology-based firms, specifically university spin-offs. Her research focuses on the development of technology-based entrepreneurial spin-offs in the Gothenburg region in Sweden, focusing on employment growth and patenting activities of corporate spin-offs versus university spin-offs in terms of employment, new job creation, growth rates and frequency of spin-off.

For this study it is interesting to go into some detail regarding the methodology, which provides insight into how to design this type of study for students wishing to develop their thesis. This is an instance of how two different samples are used. One is a sample of university spin-offs from Chalmers University of Technology in Gothenborg; the other is the sample of firms, identified and used by Utterback and Reitberger (1982), which consists of 60 'new technology-based firms' established in Sweden between 1965 and 1980. The sample of university spin-offs from Chalmers University of Technology consists of firms established before 1993, and includes a total of 193 firms (with a few acquired USOs included). This includes firms started by employees as well as ones started by students.

The results show that the majority of the USOs are very small firms, with low growth. When the annual employment growth was compared, the corporate spin-offs were found to out-perform other technology-based firms; they expanded about twice as fast as the independent start-ups and about ten times as fast as the university spin-offs. Similar results are found in studies around the world, where corporate spin-offs seem to lead to faster growth in the short term whereas a small number of university spin-offs can catch up, and grow faster, in the long term.

A different way to think about the impacts of universities on society is to see what happens to students in the future, and whether they later start companies.

Hsu et al. (2007) analysed major patterns and trends in entrepreneurship among technology-based university alumni. They studied one engineering university over a period that started in the 1930s. This study answers two related research questions: (1) Who enters entrepreneurship, and has this changed over time? (2) How does the rate of entrepreneurship vary with changes in the entrepreneurial business environment?

Hence, their definition of a university related venture follows alumni as they shift from being students into their later careers, rather than focusing upon university-employed researchers. Their results describe findings based on data from two linked datasets with information about Massachusetts Institute of Technology (MIT) alumni and founder information. The data consist of a survey of all living alumni (105 928 surveys were sent out with a response rate of 41.2 per cent).[1] Their findings show that new company formation rates by MIT alumni have grown dramatically over seven decades, and the median age of first-time entrepreneurs has gradually declined from about age 40 (1950s) to about age 30 (1990s). Women alumnae lag their male counterparts in the rate at which they become entrepreneurs, and alumni who are not US citizens enter entrepreneurship at different (usually higher) rates relative to their American classmates. This suggests that the impact of universities on industry not only occurs directly through the transfer of technical knowledge, but also the entrepreneurial activities of its alumni, increasingly soon after graduation and often years later.

3.2.3 Independent Start-ups

In all industries but especially in low-tech or traditional industries, work experience of founders may be particularly important and help drive firm formation, even for independent companies. This can be exemplified by a Danish firm within the food industry.

> All three entrepreneurs had knowledge of the industry from former work experience and the major investor, who is also the chairman of the board, also had many years of experience in convenience food market. Their insight in the market helped them identify the niche market and the potential products. (AAU – d 1.3X – CFDK1)

This illustration shows different ways in which the individual founder brings relevant knowledge into the company, and his or her ability to turn an initial idea into a viable company may be facilitated by prior work experience and relationships with a parent organization.

Even the independent start-up may be based upon an individual who can access sources of existing knowledge in society. Generally, the individual is the one to transfer this knowledge into a small start-up. Especially important ones seem to be market knowledge through industrial experience, but for companies in high-tech areas, the research and technical knowledge may be just as crucial.

3.2.4 Summary about Sources of Knowledge Inputs

This subsection focuses our attention and understanding on the antecedents of KIE. There is literature that describes issues such as the importance of endowments, the industrial dynamics of specific clusters and the relationship between entrepreneurship and technological regimes. Some of these topics thus address the overall societal and economic outputs of entrepreneurship, but our more narrow interest here is how the sources of knowledge affect the specific venture.

1. What are the sources of knowledge to the KIE venture?
    (a) Corporate spin-off.
    (b) Academic spin-off.
    (c) Independent start-up.
    (d) University spin-offs and corporate spin-off come from parent organizations that invest heavily in knowledge creation.
2. Do different sources of knowledge matter for the KIE venture?
    (a) Sources of knowledge seem to impact later performance.
    (b) Corporate spin-offs seem to be more successful initially, but possibly the academic spin-offs deliver more growth and jobs in the long run.
    (c) The results are mixed as to whether all firms obtain the positive impacts or only a handful of the most successful firms.
    (d) Many of these firms will fail in the long term, and that is the nature of starting a company based upon uncertainty. That

uncertainty can exist in the scientific, technological and creative knowledge; in the market knowledge; and in the business knowledge.

The existing literature strongly suggests that KIE founders also may have advantages if they are linked to large organizations specializing in the creation of knowledge, such as an R&D intensive large firm or a university environment – assuming that more scientific and technological opportunities are created in these types of environments, due to the overall level of investment into education and R&D. So for some types of KIE ventures, these sources of knowledge are critical for accessing resources and ideas that have an intangible value or that can be used and further applied to business contexts.

3.2.5 Questions for Discussion

1. What are the relationships and complementarities between the parent organization and the spin-off?
2. If you wanted to put together a team of founders to start a team, outline the advantages and disadvantages of hiring people with different backgrounds and experience.

3.3 CHARACTERISTICS AND TRAITS OF FOUNDERS

We now turn to the topic of the characteristics and traits of the founder. The person – or team – starting a new venture is referred to as founder. Let us start with a broad overview and turn our attention to what we know about the characteristics and traits of founders. We can then ask questions such as the ways in which knowledge intensive entrepreneurs differ from 'regular' entrepreneurs. From an economics and management perspective, the emphasis has moved away from a discussion of 'who is the entrepreneur?' to the question of what he or she actually does in the process of firm emergence (Gartner, 1993). But the question of which characteristics and traits can be distinguished as common among entrepreneurs remains of interest to many people.

Moreover, in the field of entrepreneurship, the study of characteristics and traits has been quite prevalent, including contributions from fields such as sociology, cognitive science and psychology. Across different fields, debates have been ongoing for decades about whether and how entrepreneurship should be understood as individual or societal phenomena, with debates such as whether the emergence of an entrepreneur relies upon inherent individual characteristics or whether the behaviour can be 'learned' and 'taught'. These debates rarely end; instead different authors contribute to the debates and try to strengthen one position or the other.

Large-scale empirical evidence has also been collected on these topics. Based upon the Global Entrepreneurship Monitor (GEM) survey world-wide, it is possible to empirically differentiate whether and why individuals in different countries are prepared to engage in general entrepreneurship (see http://www.gemconsortium.org). This survey asks 'potential' entrepreneurs, as well as people who actually start companies, many questions about why and how they do – or do not – start up a company.

According to a review by Garavaglia and Grieco (2005), the most common approach adopted by psychologists is aimed at investigating the correlation between defined 'personal traits' and entrepreneurial activity. This means that the research tries to identify personality traits, and then goes on to determine whether, and how, individual personality traits can be identified to lead to differences in entrepreneurial behaviour.

This stream of research builds on the work by McClelland (1961), which identifies three personality traits that stimulate change. These three personality traits are the need for power, the need for affiliation and the need for achievement. Garavaglia and Grieco (2005) review the evidence that this study (McClelland, 1961) triggered a substantial body of research on the relationship between personality and entrepreneurial behaviour that is part of sociological literature as well: among these, the role of the so-called 'internal locus of control' (Rotter, 1975); the need for autonomy, independence and personal development; personal charisma, need for approval and for following role models; welfare considerations (in terms of contributing to a sense of community); creativity and imagination (Witt, 1998); a strong belief in their ability to influence the achievement of business goals, although the risk-taking propensity of entrepreneurs does not seem to differ from managers in general (Brockhaus, 1980).

Several studies have been devoted to overconfidence, a phenomenon that has also been documented in many contexts (Kahneman and Tversky, 1982; Klayman et al., 1999). Agents may forecast competition accurately but fail in evaluating their own chances of success. Specifically, the decision to become an entrepreneur is taken even if negative industry profits are expected because of a belief in succeeding where others will fail (Camerer and Lovallo, 1999).

One classical finding (McClelland, 1961) includes the propensity of entrepreneurs to assume risk. Interestingly enough, a key finding is that those individuals who choose to become entrepreneurs tend to over-estimate their chances of success and they also tend to underestimate the risks and uncertainty involved in starting and developing a venture. They have overconfidence in their own abilities, and underestimate the risks and uncertainties involved.

If they did not think in this way and assume risk, then society as a whole would have less new ideas and organizations than otherwise, so this is positive for society. However, the individual who fails to keep a venture running or who bets money on the 'wrong' firm and loses money may not see this as positive. But they are developing resources and ideas that are valuable to society. Another way to think about this is that the entrepreneurs take new decisions and adapt along the way, thereby learning new things (and reducing uncertainties) in different dimensions like markets and technology (McKelvey and Holmèn, 2008).

The starting point is the empirical observation that some individuals take advantage of opportunities and some do not, and so why does this differ. Part of the explanation appears to be related to learning. Can one say that the opportunities seem to exist and are thus 'objective' or do they seem to be 'created' and thus subjectively identified and created through interaction with others?

Some studies have shown that social capital and network ties matter to venture creation, especially as a way to mobilize resources but also to implement the ideas. This provides one way to address issues like overconfidence, for example, as the more trust the entrepreneur has in their network contacts, the more likely they will 'trust' and act upon that knowledge. Similarly, if the entrepreneur has shared codes and language with others in the network, then this will also induce overconfidence. Bubbles are such a phenomenon.

The interesting idea here is that some of the basic characteristics and traits of the entrepreneur may not be so individually based, but they are also directly impacted by social capital and networks.

3.3.1 Risk-taking and Cognition

One relevant topic for KIE ventures is risk-taking as well as whether and how cognition is more than the risk-taking behaviour identified in the general entrepreneurship literature, and if so, how to categorize and understand how cognition affects the opportunities and knowledge used in the design of the KIE venture.

Much cognitive science has focused upon the perception of risks of entrepreneurs in general. Another way of saying this may be that entrepreneurs are ignoring the uncertainties. This type of evidence leads to interesting results about whether they believe in themselves so much that they start a company and continue running it against the odds and against evidence that suggests they may not succeed.

This is related to defining how much and whether the KIE founder trusts or even 'over-trusts' his or her own abilities and behaviour. By over-trust, Goel and Karri (2006) mean the tendency of the founder to trust in his or her own understanding more than that which is warranted, and explain this finding as how the founder uses his or her entrepreneurial characteristics in order to try to reach the goal of starting a company.

However, the evidence suggests interesting findings about the fact that we can say that cognition is more than risk-taking from the perspective of the entrepreneur. Risk-taking and 'over-trust' is of course part of the story, but there are also other aspects.

KIE founders also seem to exhibit specific personality traits related to their way of processing opportunity recognition and knowledge and of applying knowledge to develop innovations in a business context. Goel and Karri (2006) examine knowledge intensiveness in relation to 'entrepreneurs with a preference for innovation'. The KIE entrepreneur also tends to exhibit other personality characteristics. He or she tends to be non-conformist, highly self-efficient, and be high achievement oriented as well as possess a preference for innovation. The authors also find that this type of individual may become serial entrepreneurs.

Therefore, on the one hand, 'over-trust' as well as related personality characteristics seems to be a partial explanation for why people start companies, or an explanation for entrepreneurial behaviour. Conversely, this finding also suggests the need to carefully assess the validity of the information that the KIE founder is providing, as they may very well be ignoring the uncertainties involved and overestimating their personal ability to succeed.

Cognition is also very interesting in relation to innovative opportunities and knowledge, for understanding KIE ventures.

One aspect is how well they identify, learn about and mobilize to turn opportunities into a KIE venture, especially how and why they can mobilize additional resources and implement their ideas. The founders and employees often try to convince others, as well, about the viability of their ideas and the venture by providing their interpretation of events. Rae (2006) studies technology-based entrepreneurs, focusing upon entrepreneurial learning. The entrepreneur in this type of technology-based venture must bring together three themes, namely the personal and social emergence, contextual learning and the negotiated enterprise. This approach to learning assumes that interpreting what the entrepreneur is doing requires connections between the emergence of entrepreneurial identity, learning as a social and contextual process, opportunity recognition and venture formation as a negotiated activity. This means that telling narratives about the KIE venture – and especially being able to convince others of the value of something that is just starting or hard to conceptualize – is a central trait needed for creating a venture.

This type of entrepreneur may start a venture because they consider it fun and challenging.

> At this time he was 51 years old and had earned enough money by his entrepreneurial activities to retire. He was fascinated by the platform technology and its numerous fields of application and felt challenged by this risky situation that no one else of the sector felt encouraged to join this venture. (TuDo – d 1.3.x – CTGE1)

Moreover, persons who decide to become entrepreneurs are thought to have more positive associations with this role than others. They may have learned about entrepreneurship from positive role models in their environment, which appears to be a powerful way to stimulate more entrepreneurship.

Managerial thinking has often been portrayed as more routinized, with more resources to draw upon, whereas entrepreneurial thinking is thought to be more flexible and resource-constrained. Some debates touch upon whether one can really find differences in these types of thinking, as well as whether different types of individuals may be more suited for entrepreneurial ventures while others may prefer large organizations with set routines.

The cognition of the founder will likely have impacts on the company due to the close ties between how the founder thinks and how they process knowledge. These are more general properties related to knowledge structures, which influence how the individuals may be able to process and apply knowledge in a wide range of situations.

We can exemplify this by the following case of a KIE venture operating within the food industry.

> The entrepreneurs had professional competences in different fields such as business management, banking, logistic and finance, but they all had basic knowledge of the food processing industry. With the common knowledge as solid foundation, they could contribute with the expert knowledge in the respective fields to build up the new business. All three entrepreneurs had knowledge of the industry from former work experience and the major investor, who is also the chairman of the board, also had many years of experience in convenience food market. (AAU – d 1.3X – CFDK1)

Thus, in the example we see three founders with complementary prior knowledge but with industrial and market experience as their common denominator that started the company.

Risk-taking and cognition about what types of knowledge can be turned into business opportunities is a key process within entrepreneurship. The entrepreneur tries to plan, and access resources and ideas in such a way in order to reach his or her goals. However, there is uncertainty about whether the plan will work, and often about what buyers will want to purchase. Therefore, adaption is often needed. The decision and behaviour made according to the plan may or may not lead to a specific outcome as planned, but then being able to adapt is also needed and part of the process of starting a firm. Adaptation is partly about being able to find new solutions to old problems. Moreover, if the entrepreneur is overconfident, then he or she will be ignoring uncertainties and reconceptualizing a failure as a success, and this can be a useful trait, especially if it can convince others.

3.3.2   Education and Experience

Another theme to explore is how education and experience affects the opportunities identified and the knowledge used in the business model. This helps us to explore the link between the founder and the process of recognizing and acting upon opportunities.

People matter, and so it is necessary to think about who is being hired in a venture. A key insight is that individuals with knowledge tend to represent the main assets and competencies of a KIE venture. Therefore, one can study the impacts of their education and experience on starting a business, and these types of discussions are similar to the sources of knowledge discussed previously.

One question is why founders start ventures at all. What makes it more likely that some individuals will persist in designing business inputs and processes, and thereby actually start and develop a firm? Persistence matters. Key characteristics and traits appear to be their perceptions of skills, their abilities, the difficulty of the task, luck and the value of the opportunity. The evidence suggests that social aspects such as status, experience, position and network affect the opportunities identified and knowledge used in the business model of the KIE venture. The individual may have these attributes from previous experience, but it is also possible for an inexperienced entrepreneur to team up with a more experienced person to access these benefits.

One way to answer this question is to study a set of individuals active in public policy programmes, which is a type of education to start a venture. According to a study by Gatewood et al. (1995), the starting pool of subjects for this research consisted of 142 consecutive pre-venture clients, comprised of 47 women and 95 men active in a small business development centre. The centre had the explicit purpose of helping them start a business.

As part of their initial consultation, these individuals were asked to explain their decision to enter business. Two issues related to internal motivations and personal efficiency mattered a lot. One was related to internal and stable explanations for their plans for getting into business (for example, 'I have always wanted to own my own business') and the other was high scores on measures of personal efficiency; that they got things done. Moreover, in both cases, the prediction was that these types of entrepreneurs should be more likely to persist in actions that lead to successfully starting a business.

The reasons for starting a company can of course differ, but here is an illustration of how the internal motivation is linked to external conditions about getting a job.

> All three entrepreneurs got to know each other from their work in the joining technology group at a private research centre. According to Mr S they all felt intrinsically motivated by the work for the research centre but at the same time too restricted by the general conditions so that they were encouraged looking for new challenges and solutions. Above all they are interested in implementing their own ideas and think of themselves less as employees and more as entrepreneurs. Moreover, there were no career options at the research centre for the three entrepreneurs since the positions of department chiefs are limited and mainly assigned to the period of employment. (TuDo- d 1.3.X – CMG3)

They start a company partly due to a lack of other career options but also due to a clear interest in becoming entrepreneurs.

Moreover, it turns out that there are also positive effects of individuals' education and their exposure to knowledge in the likelihood of engaging in business start-up activity – but only to some extent. Having an education and skills as an individual matters a lot and that may be achieved through experiences, degrees or short courses.

As one example using the GEM survey, De Clercq and Arenius (2006) examine entrepreneurship that is highly dependent upon knowledge, relative to the general population of entrepreneurs. The analyses are based on data collected for the 2002 Global Entrepreneurship Monitor, and 4536 responses were used. More specifically, they analyse data from individuals who were between 18 to 64 years old located in Belgium and

Finland, and they examine the impact of their education and skills, and their contacts with the entrepreneurial community, on starting a company.

They analyse individuals with existing knowledge and education (which is equivalent to human capital) plus they examine individuals with a degree of exposure to external knowledge about entrepreneurship (social capital). They find that having a secondary degree positively affects the likelihood of being a nascent entrepreneur, but no effect was found for having a post-secondary degree. Hence, simply taking a Masters or PhD degree does not automatically lead to any increase in entrepreneurship. Moreover, they find a positive effect if one knows another entrepreneur on a personal basis, and this increases the likelihood of launching a new venture.

Some literature finds that the individual's perception of having the necessary skills for starting a new business is a crucial factor that increases the likelihood of business start-up activity. Bourelos et al. (2012) examine when and why academic researchers in engineering commercialize their results. Individuals who reported that they felt they had the required skills were also more likely to commercialize through patenting and starting companies. Hence, starting a venture is related to perception, educational level and knowing other entrepreneurs.

Many discussions of technology-based firms and academic spin-offs tend to almost exclusively address the technology and the opportunities related to science and technology push.

But doing so ignores the fact that technological innovations also require a clear understanding of the market. Park (2005) provides a new way to look at technology innovation by especially including a market-driven approach with a partnership between those who are really attuned to the market opportunity and the technology opportunity. Instead of focusing upon one individual who is better prepared to identify and act upon the opportunity, he proposes that we need to understand detailed interactions over time amongst groups of individuals within the venture. Even for technology-based firms, a key challenge is understanding market and business knowledge.

Having industrial experience is more likely to be the case for independent start-ups and corporate spin-offs than for academic spin-offs. The lack of managerial competencies may make it difficult to cover market and business knowledge, even if the employees are highly educated.

> The education of the entrepreneurs and the subsequent PhDs are causes of great specialization within the technology development area that is not easily transferred to managerial competences. (AAU –1.2.4, GomSpace)

The founders of academic spin-offs tend to have a more narrow experience and prior knowledge, usually limited to scientific and technical knowledge but with sparse or non-existing management and market knowledge. They can, however, partner up with an experienced entrepreneur or hire someone with industrial experience in order to overcome these problems.

3.3.3 Impact of Founder on Venture Performance

The final theme for the characteristics and traits of the founder is his or her impact upon KIE venture performance. This is a long-term impact which can also be identified in this initial phase of designing business inputs and processes, but here the question is whether the impact can be traced to a much later phase of the KIE venture.

Thus, another interesting issue is whether and how the founder affects the later performance of the KIE venture. If no, then anyone can be an entrepreneur. If yes, then one ought to be careful to partner with another founder with particular characteristics and traits. Indeed, there is no straightforward answer. The evidence is mixed and sometimes contradictory, but still provides expectations and predictions about how founders impact performance in different ways.

How should one set up the company? One question is whether the founder, and later manager, of a KIE venture should be a generalist or a specialist, that is, whether one person should assume multiple roles or whether each person should have a very defined role. One way to study this is to examine three different roles, which appear in most KIE ventures, namely the entrepreneurial, managerial and technical-functional roles. These roles seem particularly important in later managerial stages, but also affect the initial start-up of the company.

- The entrepreneurial role should focus upon the flexibility and access to new ideas and resources. This requires adaptability and creativity.
- The managerial role should focus upon coordinating and using existing resource to deliver goals. This requires conceptual, interpersonal and political competence.

- The technical-functional role is to understand what types of technologies and functions are necessary for the idea to be commercialized. This requires that the individual is able to use the tools or procedures required in his or her specialized field.

So, is it better to have one individual with all roles or three individuals, each taking on one role? Chandler and Jansen (1992) studied manufacturing and service firms, where the founder as a minimum had a college degree, in order to study the relationships between founders' characteristics and venture performance. Their study was based upon a questionnaire to 134 founders (33.8 per cent response rate), using self-evaluations of their own competencies according to these three roles. They asked questions in the survey about founder characteristics (which included biographical data and self-reported competences) as well as firm performance. They defined firm performance or success in terms of firms that show higher levels of growth and earnings.

Interestingly enough, their questionnaire showed the differences between what is self-reported and what one could find through other data, especially if one looked over time. Two dimensions of venture performance were analysed using quantitative data, namely growth and profitability. For initial phases of the venture, the most successful founders in terms of firm performance also rated themselves as competent in the entrepreneurial, managerial and technical-functional roles. These are the competent generalists. Later, however, in the next phase, it appears that the venture needs specialists, so that different people should be recruited for roles.

Entrepreneurial experience and how it affects performance can be exemplified through two cases, the first being a Greek start-up within the food industry and the second being a German academic spin-off in the textile industry.

Mr KS was an entrepreneur long before the establishment of CFGR2. He actually has been an experienced entrepreneur for more than 40 years. He is an economist. He was running a construction company, when in 1974 he turned to tomato processing, since it was one of the region's main cultivations. In 1982 he engages a young chemist who later marries his daughter and becomes partner – Mr T. Meanwhile his son KJ takes his diploma in economics and enters the firm in the end of the decade of 1990s. In 2000, they all decide to abandon the tomato product foreseeing its slow death. In 2001 a cooperative grain mill went to auction. The family bought it and in June 2002 the first conventional wheat flour was produced. (LIE-NTUAA – d. 1.3.x – CFGR2)

Mr L has been an experienced entrepreneur for 36 years. He has already founded fourteen companies in different sectors such as IT, electronics or leasing services but had no business experience in the textile industry so far. Mr L has no formal education. He broke up the secondary education and a professional education as a mechanician, worked as a vendor and purchaser without any formal commercial apprenticeship. He picked up his commercial know-how on the job. In the age of 22 he founded his first company. Before the establishment of CTGE1 Mr L sold a former company in the electronics sector to a leading company for metal fittings and took a timeout from business. Mr L is considered as creative and as a professional in marketing and sales. He widened the business strategy for consumer products which is supposed to lead to the main volume of sales in a few years by licensing to big manufacturers. Moreover, he organised the investors for commercialising the new fibres from his social network. The motivation of Mr L can be described as intrinsic. (TuDo – d 1.3.x – CTGE1)

These illustrations give insight into how the KIE venture performance can change over time. Even experienced founders may not be able to keep the venture going over a long time period, or else they may decide to close one line of business to concentrate on another.

Experience can impact performance in different ways. By experience, we mean many different things, including a wide range from experience with the technology, with the industry and the market, and with the experience of starting and running other ventures.

3.3.4 Summary about Characteristics and Traits of Founders

This subsection gives insight into whether, and how, the individual – including their personality traits and previous experience – will play a key role in understanding the development and exploitation of opportunities in a particular KIE venture.

1. Do KIE ventures exhibit specific characteristics and traits – as compared to entrepreneurship in general?
    (a) Characteristics of general entrepreneurs also apply to KIE, such as risk-taking, overconfidence and building narratives towards others.
    (b) They may be more extreme, however, in that they act under conditions of great uncertainty about what they can do – and what others expect – in terms of science, technological and creative knowledge, in terms of market knowledge and in terms of business knowledge.
2. What differentiates the knowledge intensive entrepreneur?

(a)	Networks, social capital to access market and technological opportunities.
(b)	In specific cases, experience and education matter.
(c)	Designing the venture, done by relating the founder's ability to perceive opportunity recognition with external factors such as luck, technology, market growth and so on.
3.	Can differences be observed that affect venture performance?
(a)	Yes, many of them related to social capital and networks.

Do these factors matter, and interact, in ways that influence future venture performance? The results suggest yes. One reason why it matters which person is the founder is that they often have certain characteristics and traits.

- Cognitive biases. These have to do with the characteristics of overconfidence in their own abilities, illusion of control and often experience, which shapes how they develop the firm.
- Risk perception. This has to do with an underestimation of the risks involved, which conversely helps drive the desire to exploit entrepreneurial opportunities.
- Social capital. This has to do with network and societal aspects, such as knowing people, trust, shared codes and language that help to access resources and ideas.

These variables interact in ways that affect the development of a KIE venture.

3.3.5 Questions for Discussion

1.	What characteristics do you think to be the most likely to look for, but also important for future success, if you were a founder choosing a partner to become co-founder?
2.	Do you think that entrepreneurs are 'born' with these personality characteristics and cognition? Or can they be 'formed' and 'trained' through experience? Why or why not?
3.	How much can you 'trust' what a founder of a KIE venture tells you?
4.	Why do the education, skills and understanding of the role of the entrepreneur affect the start-up phase?
5.	Which initial assets and competencies of academic spin-offs will affect the business inputs and resources?

3.4 FINANCING

The study of financing focuses on the manner in which the venture can obtain sufficient types and quantities of financing to mobilize resources and exploit the innovative opportunities. Mobilizing finance is critical for designing a knowledge intensive venture. Financing generally comes from outside these firms, given that they do not have enough sales to generate sufficient income to cover costs.

The questions that we are interested in, in relation to KIE ventures, are: What are the sources of financing, especially which alternatives exist to venture capital? What is the role of venture capital? Are those alternatives organized through public policy and corporate venture capital likely to affect the types of companies financed?

Generally speaking, financing is an area that has received a lot of attention in the field of entrepreneurship as well as in relation to public policy implications. Moreover, we would expect that KIE ventures are likely to be trying to obtain financing for more risky ventures in contrast to general entrepreneurship. The most valuable assets may be of an intangible nature such as knowledge, experience and creativity, making it difficult to articulate the possible value of future business models, which is necessary to obtain financing.

Note that although we have put financing as an input, financing is not only a one-off need during formation, but something that runs through the management and development processes. Relevant aspects of financing that have been identified in the literature include – but are not limited to – the sources of financing, the different types of risk involved in finance, the subsequent effects upon the venture as well as the time frame and process into which different types of financing are needed.

A key insight is that the same company may need different amounts of investment through financing at different times. It is difficult and often costly to obtain enough money to do everything that the company has set out to do, given the limited resources. Most studies suggest that these types of ventures have difficulties in obtaining sufficient resources. Empirical cases, such as those found in the companion case study book (McKelvey and Lassen, 2013), also illustrate the trade-offs and need to change direction that occur when the company suddenly obtains a lot of financing – or runs out of money.

3.4.1 Types of Financing

Although there are many types of financing available, there are multiple ways for risk financing, such as debt, including direct loans and loan guarantees; equity, including business angels and venture capital; and government grants.

According to results from the AEGIS Survey (2012), the use of venture capital in Europe in the very early stages of the venture creation is quite limited. In only 5 per cent of the cases had venture capital been a part of the start-up phase, whereas 92 per cent of the KIE ventures had had to rely on their own financial resources.

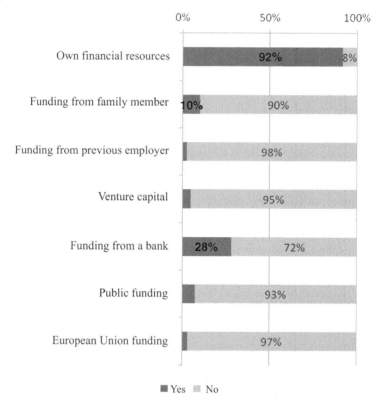

Figure 3.2   Sources of funding in KIE ventures

These responses demonstrate an important point about these processes and phenomena of KIE – that the entrepreneurs' own financial resources or family resources are quite important, and that even funding from banks plays a significant role in KIE ventures. Naturally, these resources tend to be limited, and may make it difficult to expand the venture or obtain enough financing to do both R&D and sales simultaneously.

Possibly, Figure 3.2 also illustrates a fundamental problem in the set-up of the European venture capital industry in that few KIE ventures obtain money from them. Other research suggests that venture capital is highly important, both in financial terms and in terms of access to expertise that follows – but the venture capitalists are reluctant to invest in the early stages due to higher levels of uncertainty and potential risks of failure.

We may think about this lack of venture capital and find a possible explanation through the framework proposed by Ben-Ari and Vonortas (2007). This is primarily a conceptual paper, focused primarily upon new technology-based firms. The term 'new technology-based firm' (NTBF) tended to dominate earlier literature by taking the perspective that knowledge-based economies are driven by the creation and expansion of new economic activities in the high-tech and knowledge intensive sectors and by the diffusion of new technologies within the economy.

These types of ventures have limited options for obtaining financing from external sources. This is due to the following characteristics: they have little or no collateral; their assets tend to be intangible; and the value of their innovation is hard to calculate. Therefore, for these reasons, entrepreneurs in the more knowledge intensive fields tend to rely largely on equity financing. This is a more 'patient' form of capital for early stage operations with returns linked directly to firm earnings.

Ben-Ari and Vonortas's (2007) findings suggest that the amount of capital raised by venture capital firms will depend heavily on external factors. These include the existence of effective exit mechanisms, such as IPOs and mergers and acquisitions (M&As) as well as the availability of enterprises to invest locally. As the amount of capital in venture capital funds increases, these types of financers should show less interest in small, risky investments and more interest in larger, safer deals.

In recent years, the number of IPOs has decreased dramatically, as have the number of publicly owned companies listed on the stock market. Surrounding the information technology (IT) bubble centred around 2000, many investors wanted to exit through IPOs and become rich by selling their share. It can become more difficult for the venture to find this type of financing in times when fewer companies lead to IPOs or in turbulent times.

3.4.2 Venture Capital

Much research on financing has focused upon venture capital. It is likely that a number of KIE ventures have obtained venture capital, which has offered a way to access resources and expand or pursue innovative opportunities.

Companies that have received venture capital have been highly successful in at least some phases including well-known brands such as:

- Starbucks Corporation
- Whole Foods Market, Inc.
- eBay
- Microsoft
- Intel Corporation
- Apple Inc.
- Google
- Facebook.

The term venture capital in the literature is applied to several types of investment entities. Landström (2007) categorizes research on venture capital by the three types of venture capitalists, namely informal venture capitalists, formal venture capitalists and corporate venture capitalists. Generally, people mean formal venture capitalists when they use the term venture capital, but the other two forms also finance significant development work.

Informal venture capital is known as business angels, and these are private individuals with a high net worth who invest in new ventures. They often have previous successful entrepreneurial ventures behind them and a significant network of contacts within their areas of business. Private investors invest their own money and not the money of a large fund, although groups of business angels may invest together.

Venture capital is generally viewed as a response to the lack of capital supply for companies facing high risks, where bank loans and other forms of capital are difficult to obtain or only provide small amounts relative to total needs. The high risk is largely due to uncertainties in the direction and speed that development of the company may take in the future, and the risk of significant information asymmetries between company managers and potential investors.

In particular, technology-based firms such as academic spin-offs and science-based firms such as those in biotechnology may require years of investment in development work before products are sold (McKelvey, 1996). Other types of KIE may have lower up-front development costs but still require external financing to exploit the opportunities that they have identified because without funding they cannot be started.

Formal venture capitalists are the most commonly discussed entity. A formal venture capitalist has to fulfil five characteristics, as defined by Metrick (2006):

- A venture capitalist is a financial intermediary, meaning that it takes the investors' capital and invests it directly in portfolio companies.
- A venture capitalist invests only in private companies. This means that once the investments are made, the companies cannot be immediately traded on a public exchange.
- A venture capitalist takes an active role in monitoring and helping the companies in its portfolio.
- A venture capitalist's primary goal is to maximize its financial return by exiting investments through a trade sale or IPO.
- A venture capitalist invests to fund the internal growth of companies.

The venture capitalist is able to exert considerable influence on how the company is managed and the likelihood for successful growth due to its unique financial position in the KIE ventures, which are called portfolio firms. There may also be stormy relationships between the venture and the incoming venture capitalist, such as in cases when the venture capitalist decides to move out the existing founder and bring in an experienced manager to run the company.

The most common way in which venture capitalists secure their interests is by taking a seat on the board. Gupta (2004) says that 'Venture capitalists often want to dictate the board structure in companies they invest in, including size, number of representatives from each constituency, the inclusion of independent board members and veto rights in certain decisions.' Furthermore Huse (2007) states that a company's board of directors can work as a group of professional advisors to a company and the composition of the board will in these cases reflect and represent the needs of the company.

There are interesting questions about how the founders' own experiences and social networks affect their ability to obtain financing. Atherton (2009) studied 26 cases of new venture creation, and focused upon the experiential nature of financing. In contrast to existing finance literature, which tends to refer to efficiency and economic rationales underpinning such choices, his study explored how prior experience and networks help the venture find money.

A key implication of this analysis is an alternative explanation for sources of funding. The findings suggest that prior knowledge and experience of the founder of a new venture, as well as the relational capital as represented by established networks and existing relationships, affect the types of finance and the amount of capital that the new venture could acquire.

New venture founders tend to bundle multiple sources of finance into a single package of funding for the new venture. This could be to spread risk amongst funders or to ensure that the new venture is not overly reliant on a single source. An illustration of how this happens can be seen in this case.

> By middle 2007, [the original founder] and Mr. CC met through common friends. 'I immediately got interested in the idea. It seemed very interesting', says Mr. CC. But he thought the project needed a strategic plan and a financial partner. From his network he knew Mr. AM who owned a venture capital company and who got interested in the project, both as an investor and as a partner.

Thus, in this case the venture capitalist was outside the initial network, but was encouraged to join the founding team and provide part of the start-up capital.

3.4.3 Corporate Venture Capital (CVC)

Large firms are also involved in financing risky ventures, either with the intention of retaining control in-house of the new company or with the intention of finding alternative uses for interesting in-house ideas. Corporations use a variety of approaches to innovation, including internal R&D, incubation of new businesses, and strategic investments and alliances. Many emphasize a strategy of 'open innovation' to bring external sources of innovation into the firm. Given the success of market-based venture capital in creating new entrepreneurial companies and technologies, corporations have also looked to that model as yet another approach to innovation.

Corporate venture capital (CVC) may be defined as programmes in established firms that make investments in entrepreneurial companies. Typically, a CVC makes a financial investment – just as independent venture capital does – and receives a minority equity stake in the entrepreneurial company. In return, the corporation gains an insight into both new technologies and strategically complementary companies that may become strategic partners.

While the main objective is generally financial return on ideas developed in-house, CVCs can have a strategic objective as well in developing a spin-off that is complementary to large, existing companies. That strategic objective may include leveraging external sources of innovation, bringing new ideas and technologies into the company or taking 'real options' on technologies and business models by investing in a wider array of technologies or business directions than the company can itself pursue.

The strengths of CVCs is, in particular, that corporate investors have access, on the one hand, to technological, market and business knowledge that independent venture funds rarely possess (Maula and Murray, 2000) and, on the other, to more material corporate facilities such as distribution channels and R&D opportunities. Such resources broaden the range of value-creating services that corporate investors can provide for their portfolio firms.

Therefore, in this sense, Gompers and Lerner (1998), come to the conclusion that corporate venture capital is at least as successful as venture capital, if first there is possible access and ownership to technical and market know-how in the company, and second, the access to important resources of the company is established. Similarly, Brody and Ehrlich (1998) point out that another success factor of corporate venture capital is that the parent company has to secure access to its resources, contact persons, technology and innovative know-how by the involvement of the corporation. The start-up company gets additional resources and ideas than if it were an independent start-up.

According to the National Venture Capital Association (NVCA) this tendency is particularly visible among CVCs in general, and in a study published by the NVCA in 2009, it illustrated that CVCs tend to favour investments in the later stages of the venture development (Figure 3.3).

The reason for such distribution could potentially be found in the objective of CVCs, that is, to bring new ideas and technologies into the company. This requires that the technology is proven to have a certain potential, and the investments target the growth and maturing stages of the technology.

There are considerable debates about the relative effectiveness of corporate venturing, and how it may relate to, or compete with, venture capital. Corporate venturing is sometimes said to be the most productive as a path to superior corporate performance when practised in a strategic manner. But this is not easy.

Considerable ambiguity exists concerning what it means to strategically pursue CVC, given the failure of many companies to do so in their organizational practice. Covin and Miles (2007) provide a critical analysis of corporate venturing in large corporations, where the research focuses on organizations investing heavily in R&D and venturing. They

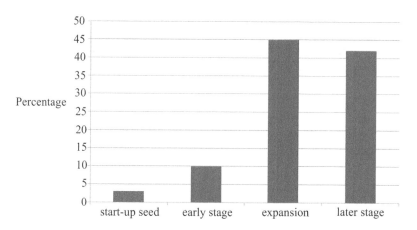

Figure 3.3   CVC investment focus

suggest that companies may make inefficient decisions, and fund ideas that are not likely to survive on the market.

Part of the literature describes CVC in relation to managed corporate spin-outs, referring to how large corporations can provide financing and other resources to form new ventures based upon technology and R&D. Chesbrough (2000) and Chesbrough and Socolof (2003) investigate corporate venturing in R&D intensive companies. Examples are taken from 19 ventures such as Lucent New Ventures Group (NVG), Intel, 3M, Raychem, Thermo-Electron and Xerox. The focus is on types of new ventures that are R&D- or technology-driven. Their findings suggest that the recent surge in private venture capital makes the design of corporate ventures even more problematic as these ventures must compete with independent venture capital for entrepreneurial talent latent in the firm.

Lucent's NVG represents an organizational structure that illustrates how corporate venture structures can be designed in this new environment. The organization tries to balance many aspects of private venture capital with other aspects of its corporate mission. Lucent New Ventures Group is consciously a hybrid, lying between a pure venture capital model and a pure corporate development model. It works closely with Lucent's businesses, yet it retains an independent ability to select technologies and take them to market. Thus, on the one hand, it seeks to exploit Lucent's resources to the fullest but, on the other hand, is free to pursue whatever business model it wishes to use for a new venture. This has implications for human resources management. Its managers are compensated for their return on their investment and even reacquired ventures are purchased at market prices.

The authors' findings suggest that large companies with significant internal R&D capabilities are searching for mechanisms to create more value out of their R&D investment. Finding ways to start new ventures can thus be key for renewing a large company. Developing spin-off ventures based upon technology that will be underutilized in the company could be a vehicle for stimulating more rapid commercialization of the huge investments in R&D.

The implication of these lines of research is that large established companies can also stimulate renewal through new ventures but in a way that exploits their advantages rather than simply competing with venture capital for ideas.

Time and financing are also highly interrelated issues. Financing of new ventures is difficult in the long term. Lucent's and Bell's experiences illustrate a growing realization within corporations that creating new ventures out of internal technology must be managed for the long term if it is to be sustained through down phases in the corporate and industry life cycle. It takes time to develop the venture creation expertise in the portfolio management team and the returns from these activities will be lumpy and difficult to predict.

Thus, when careful financial planning and management is absent, companies may vacillate, entering into venture creation when times are good, only to abandon it when times are bad. Partnering with external private equity specialists provides corporations with one alternative to this erratic behaviour by transferring most of the risks and governance to the private equity players. This demonstrates some of the difficulties of sustained financing through CVC over business cycles and industry life cycles.

Another way to discuss the relationship between large companies and small companies is through what Dittmar (2004) calls managed spin-out firms. He argues that in a spin-off process, the parent divides the assets of the firm and chooses the capital structure for the new, stand-alone entity, and hence it is important to evaluate the question: Do firms have an optimal or target capital structure and, if so, do they lever the firm to coincide with this target? This approach suggests that the strategy of the parent firm – which is assumed to be both large and existing – helps determine the financing of the new venture.

Dittmar (2004) used a sample consisting of 155 subsidiaries spun off from large corporations in 150 different events announced between 1983 and 1995. The purpose was to investigate how firms determine their capital structure. He found that the subsidiary has a leverage ratio that is lower than that of the parent firm but similar to that of a comparable independent start-up. Growth opportunities are the primary determinant of the subsidiary's leverage. Profitability has no impact on leverage choice. These results support the predictions of the trade-off theory of capital structure and provide insight into why previous studies find a negative relation between leverage and profitability. Specifically, growth is negatively related and collateral value is positively related to leverage choice. Further, profitability is not inversely related to leverage choice and is positively related to the difference in a firm's actual and predicted leverage ratio.

The design principles for CVC could be beneficial to large companies, especially ones that invest heavily in R&D. These potential advantages include: an indefinite time horizon; the ability to commit very large sums of capital; the ability to coordinate complementarities with non-tradable corporate assets; and the ability to retain greater group and organizational learning from failed venture experiences.

3.4.4 Summary about Financing

Three main points are:

- KIE ventures are financed in a variety of ways, including debt and equity financing.
- KIE ventures in peripheral locations, in markets that are ill-defined and in early stage technologies can have increasing difficulties in accessing equity financing.
- Much is not yet completely understood about financing. Research should focus on the relative importance and role of sources of financing that are not (necessarily) organized through the market, such as business angels, private savings including mortgages and investments from family members.

1. What are the alternatives to venture capital?
   (a) Individual and family financing is the most common.
   (b) Venture capital remains important to KIE, especially for ones heavily reliant upon technology and science.
   (c) KIE have the same range of alternatives as other entrepreneurs, but their firms have no credit history, and often unclear products and future revenues. Hence they exhibit certain characteristics that tend to limit financing sources.
2. What are the large-scale financing alternatives from existing large companies?

(a) Corporate venture capital represents one alternative to market-based venture capital.

(b) For corporate venture capital (CVC), the KIE has to be spun-out from a larger firm, which often invests in R&D and has skilled employees.

(c) CVC represent financing alternatives for certain sub-groups of KIE ventures, and these generally retain many relationships with the existing company.

The availability of financing is related to the types of market and technological opportunities being exploited by the KIE. This partly reflects the nature of the venture. These ventures rarely exploit market asymmetries that are visible to many, which is one classical definition of the role of an entrepreneur. Our proposition thus implies that the opportunities that may be perceived by the knowledge intensive entrepreneur may not be visible to others, making it difficult to convince others of the potential future benefits. If you can't convince others of the benefits, then it is difficult to obtain financing. This is probably a major reason why so many ventures are self-financed.

Financing relies upon someone believing in the future market potential and attractiveness of what are probably future products and services, and not something that already exists. The reasons why the opportunities are not visible have to do with such aspects as the role of intangibles, risk/uncertainty and ability to appropriate returns to knowledge through commercialization.

Moreover, the business models of these types of firms may also not be well articulated, or change rapidly, depending upon their perception of the match between the technological knowledge and the potential application of that knowledge to different industries, products, processes and services. Still, without financing, the venture cannot grow.

3.4.5 Questions for Discussion

1. Which type of financing can be available?
2. Discuss the pros and cons of the different types of financing, including but not limited to venture capital.
3. Discuss how you would gain access to the different types of venture capital, if you were starting a venture.

3.5 SOCIETAL INFLUENCES AND PUBLIC POLICY

A final variable is societal influences and public policy. These are broader influences that affect the ability of the KIE venture to access resources and ideas. We follow two specific examples, namely incubators and clusters that illustrate the real choices facing decision-makers.

For incubators, the American National Business Incubation Association (NBIA) describes incubation as a dynamic process of business enterprise development. The term refers to an interactive development process where the aim is to encourage people to start their own business and to support start-up companies in the development of innovative products.

Aaboen (2009) describes the role of incubators for KIE as the idea that public policy should seek an effective means to link technology, capital and know-how in order to leverage entrepreneurial talent, accelerate the development of new companies, and thus speed the exploitation of technology. Hence, a true incubator is not only office space with a shared secretary and a common financial support. Besides accommodation, an incubator should offer services such as hands-on management, access to finance (mainly through links with seed capital funds or business angels), legal advice, operational know-how and access to new markets. This is a rather broad definition of incubators.

Moreover, we should ask about the purpose of public policy in order to understand the impact of these societal influences on the development of KIE. Do we want entrepreneurs, regardless of type and industry? Or should public policy stimulate specific types of entrepreneurs? A good classification of this can be found in Grimaldi and Grandi (2005), based on a study of eight Italian incubators. They argue that two very different overall purposes of incubators exist.

The purpose of the first type of incubators lies in the capacity to reduce start-up costs for small entrepreneurial initiatives, targeting local markets, more anchored to the old economy, looking for local visibility and local contacts with public and private institutions, requiring small amounts of capital to start up and valuing the provision of logistical assets.

The purpose of the second type of incubators lies in their ability to accelerate the start-up process of highly promising entrepreneurial initiatives, attractive in terms of size of investments, fast and aggressive and looking for high-value services. (Thus this model includes access to advanced technology, market, managerial knowledge and competencies and day-to-day operational support).

Thus, a key issue for public policy is to decide what types of firms they wish to stimulate. And public policy can then decide about the differing foci of different types of incubators, even if they all face the same overall goal of stimulating technology.

Using this type of wide categorization, we can use the main rationale, main objective and main strengths, in order to map different types of incubators into four categories:

1. Business Innovation Centres (BICs)
2. University Business Incubators (UBIs)
3. Independent Private Incubators (IPIs)
4. Corporate Private Incubators (CPIs).

Table 3.1 illustrates how the different types of incubators are based on various rationales, how they serve different purposes and have different strengths in terms of how they affect KIE and ventures creation.

Table 3.1   The roles of different types of incubators

	Main rationale	Main objective	Main strength
BICs Public incubation	BICs are developed to be public/institutional operators with economic development objectives (to boost employment and economic/ technological growth), and rely mainly on public resources.	The incubating activity of BICs consists in offering a set of basic services to tenant companies, including the provision of space, infrastructure, communication channels, and information about external financing opportunities, visibility, etc.	Many local economic development agencies, government and other public institutions have adopted incubators. This creates a large and general focus on venture creation, independent of sector/ industry/technology focus.
UBIs Public incubation	UBIs are developed in recognition of the fact that universities play an important and direct entrepreneurial role in generating and spreading scientific and technological knowledge.	Government policy-makers view science as a vehicle for energizing national and regional economies and UBIs are a mechanism for universities to lend resources, faculty time and talent to economic development efforts.	Transfer of scientific and technological knowledge from universities to companies.

Table 3.1   Continued

	Main rationale	Main objective	Main strengths
IPIs Private incubation	IPIs are developed as a response to the fact that specialized and targeted incubation of ventures is a profitable service market, which emphasizes the speed to market, quick access to capital, synergy, network, strategic cohesiveness of the venture.	The purpose of for-profit incubators is to quickly create new ventures and in return take a portion of equity in the new venture as fees. IPIs emphasize the efficient completion of the entrepreneurs' business models, the provision of experienced operation staff, recruiting mechanisms, networks of relations with key strategic actors for all aspects of business relationships with strategic partners not ordinarily motivated to deal with smaller accounts.	IPIs plan and carry out highly specialized incubation processes, which speeds up the process of venture creation.
CPIs Private incubation	CPIs are developed mainly based on the rationale that the efficient use of knowledge developed internally in existing organizations may be exploited in a more profitable manner through a separate business unit or venture than by being integrated into the main strategic activities of the parent organization.	CPIs are incubators owned and set up by large companies with the aim of supporting the emergence of new independent business units. These new business units (corporate spin-offs) usually originate from research project spill-over (carried out within parent organizations). It is quite common for the parent organization to retain a degree of control over the new ventures by holding equity stake.	Intervenes during the early stages (business concept definition) of the venture creation, as well as when the business has already been launched and needs specific injections of capital or know-how.

The distinction between the four different types of incubators in Table 3.1 reflects, to a certain degree, the two overall differences in purpose.

The public incubators BICs and UBIs generally have a higher focus on reducing start-up costs and promoting entrepreneurial activity in local areas, whereas the privately held incubators focus on accelerating the start-up process and reducing time-to-profit. This may to some extent also reflect the nature of public versus private policy, where public policy aims at creating the foundations of long-term sustainability either regionally or nationally, and private policy often favours the creation of more short-term oriented profits.

However, as with all generalizations, it is important to emphasize that such overall distinction will not be valid in all cases. Particularly when we focus on KIE-oriented incubators, the dynamic requirements of such ventures also spark further development of the incubators that support them. As such, we are increasingly seeing collaboration and even mergers between UBIs and IPIs, where the common purpose is to develop highly specialized venture incubation for KIE ventures with special needs, in terms of technology development, market development, venture capital or network contacts.

3.5.1 Clusters

If we look especially at high-tech firms, there seems to be a strong link between financing and clustering of firms within a geographical area, like a town or region.

Regional agglomeration and stimulating clusters has been a huge topic within public policy and research. Regionally, close network relationships and access to venture capital financing have been demonstrated as vital for the formation of ventures, with a strong emphasis on venture capital in the so-called Silicon model of development. The Silicon model means that many small high-tech firms are started up in a limited geographical area, with an assumption that many receive venture capital to form and develop the company. This seems to assume that independent and autonomous companies can develop using external financing, and often with some assumption of strong geographical clustering.

However, others argue that large companies are key to starting up related companies in a region, which has been shown for such diverse industries as automobile and laser.

As to the Silicon Valley story, Keeble and Oakey (1998) have argued that in Silicon Valley the main reasons for high-technology growth were the presence of input linkage economies, local venture capital and a pool of skilled labour, together with corporate spin-offs from existing businesses. This type of reasoning suggests that while companies depend upon financing, regional development is driven by more factors than simply financing.

Public policy has also been very active in trying to develop regional clusters and help start-up companies within a region. For example, one KIE venture explained:

> The company made use of a funding program called EXIST-SEED for academic start-ups in 2006/07 kick starting formal establishment as a legal entity and building up production facilities. This program is the standard tool of the technology transfer office of the University of Kassel. It has a competitive selection process of the applicants which guarantees a certain quality of the funded ideas. According to the founders the grant was vital for the firm and they do not know if they would have pursued establishment of the firm without it. (MPI d 1.3.X, CFGE2)

We can also give an example of how a country has used different types of incubators to stimulate high-tech clusters. Israel has been particularly successful in stimulating high-tech companies. An interesting question is thus whether public policy can help pull this type of development into peripheral regions. Avnimelech et al. (2007) studied high-tech clusters and the diffusion of high-tech activities towards more peripheral areas in Israel. Their findings are based on the Israeli experience with two specific government programmes: Yozma, which triggered the emergence of the venture capital industry, and compared this to the technological incubators programme.

These two public policy programmes had significant impact on the development of the high-tech cluster in Israel. While venture capital has a positive impact on the growth and strength of high-tech clusters, it also has significant drawbacks, such as narrow geographical distribution of high-tech activities and narrow technological diversification. Their empirical work is based on a population of 3747 Israeli high-tech firms established between 1991 and 2004.

This raises interesting results for other countries and regions wanting to start incubators. The findings suggest that while venture capital-backed firms have higher success rates, their activities are more concentrated in central areas, hence increasing the economic gap between central areas and peripheral areas. In contrast, the technological incubators proved successful in attracting activity to peripheral areas and to less popular technologies, but their success rates are very low. Finally, the findings suggest that incubator graduates that received venture capital financing had significantly improved results.

As could be expected, in some countries European Union (EU) grants can be found to play an important role for developing the ventures:

As many innovative firms in Poland are currently successful partially thanks to EU grants they did not have enough money e.g. to do good marketing of the innovation without the grant. (CASE, d. 2.2.X, Desmart)

This illustration suggests that available public policy financing is crucial for each KIE venture, even though the quote also suggests that financing remains a difficult challenge for these types of firms. However, this type of quote gives us no information about whether venture capital funding had been more efficient than public policy financing, but obviously venture capital or the alternative forms discussed above were not available to this firm. Public policy-makers have to make decisions based on available information, and may choose to support a wider range of firms than the market will support.

Lerner (2009) raises a more critical voice about the potential role of government in boosting entrepreneurship and venture capital, using insights and descriptive data from many regions and policy interventions around the globe and based upon conceptual reasoning. He discusses new enterprises in general, but primarily high-tech companies and clusters, given the foci of venture capital into these industries. He explains how public intervention into venture capital is based upon premises, including the recognized role of technological innovation as stimulating economic growth and the particular part played by venture capital.

The Silicon Valley example is again examined, but here from the perspective of the role of public policy as a catalyst for the broader changes ongoing in the region. He also brings up examples of the American Research and Development (ARD) and the later Small Business Investment Companies (SBICs). They were means of bringing together capital in ways that made it possible for entrepreneurs to obtain capital to commercialize ideas. He finds that although public policy can play a catalytic role in stimulating growth, much policy fails and ends with wasting public money.

Public policy can impact the formation of new ventures, including a wider distribution of regions and technologies. However, the findings also raise important issues about the complex relationships between the success of the ventures, venture capital and public policy initiatives like incubators. Some studies find that public monies may be 'wasted' if they are supporting the same high-tech companies financed by venture capital. Several important areas of additional research can follow upon the inter-relatedness of public-private financing and upon the differential success rates of different types of financing.

Another aspect of clustering is how services and manufacturing interact with each other. The evidence about outside advice and planning suggests that they can promote the formation of new enterprises and increase their success with product planning, respectively. Even if the founders face an uncertain and ambiguous context, these tools help structure the opportunities being exploited as well as the use of internal resources when forming the venture.

This means that these services are valuable. Garcia-Quevedo and Mas-Verdu (2008) investigate collaboration between knowledge intensive services (KIS) and high-tech firms. They argue that service providers are key players in the creation and commercialization of new products, processes and services, and argue that they are fundamental as carriers and creators of both technological and organizational innovation. Reporting from a database of more than 2000 firms and with the use of binary models, these two authors analyse the factors that explain the use of KIS by small- and medium-sized firms. Specifically, the services supplied by technological centres with the purpose of improving regional innovative potential are examined. The results show that demand for services increases with the size of the user firms. Spatial proximity between the user and the supplier of the KIS also seems to be a relevant factor. Other variables such as age, sector, innovation level and exports are examined.

Their results seem particularly relevant because of their importance for the definition of public policy. The study identifies, on the one hand, the existence of a certain threshold in terms of firm size as well as technological level in order for a firm to be able to make efficient use of KIS. Conversely, the study stresses the importance of proximity, both geographical and functional (sectoral), between the suppliers and users of the services.

3.5.2   Summary about Societal Influences and Public Policy

Societal influences and public policy offer different types of resources and ideas as inputs to the creation of a KIE venture. They can offer financing, even on competing terms with venture capital, but generally the objective of public policy is to stimulate KIE in a broader range of technologies or geographical areas than the market per se would support.

1.   What four categories of incubators can be identified based upon their main rationale, objective and advantages?
      (a) Business Innovation Centres (BICs).
      (b) University Business Incubators (UBIs).
      (c) Independent Private Incubators (IPIs).
      (d) Corporate Private Incubators (CPIs).
2.   How does public policy interact with geographical clustering?

(a) Public policy can help diffuse financing and advice to firms that would not obtain it on the market.
(b) KIS and manufacturing seem to gain advantages from being geographically clustered.

One key issue for policy-makers is to decide whether the objective is to stimulate the start-up of all types of entrepreneurship or whether to focus upon a particular type, such as KIE ventures. This matters in terms of the different rationales and types of services that need to be provided.

3.5.3 Questions for Discussion

1. If you were running a KIE service company, what are the main benefits and services that you would need from an incubator?
2. Is it a good use of public money to support firms that cannot obtain it from the market? Why or why not?

3.6 CONCLUDING REMARKS

A crucial part of entrepreneurship is understanding how and why firms can access resources and ideas, even before a KIE venture is formed.

This chapter has focused on inputs, and particularly on accessing resources and ideas that are needed as inputs to the processes and phenomena before the venture is created.

Accessing inputs, which are resources and ideas, is crucial to starting the company. This phase refers to the processes and phenomena before the venture is created. The emphasis is on how and why to use resources and ideas that are linked to the founder or that can be transferred from the ecosystem and external environment to the venture. The KIE venture often draws upon existing organizations, and this leads to many decisions about how and why to use them to balance planning and emergent opportunities.

This chapter has addressed the origins of and important inputs to KIE, and related this to the broader ecosystem and societal context.

There are clear reasons – and one of the contributions of this book – that we start by discussing business founding, and inputs and resources rather than on the internal processes of business plans. The reason is that modern entrepreneurship literature has found that the individual entrepreneur – or firm – relies upon inputs and resources from other actors in society, and we feel this is an interesting line of thought to further pursue.

Moreover, the source, quality and type of inputs and resources tend to influence the success of these types of firms as much as the internal management processes functioning in the next phase.

NOTE

1. Of them, 7798 individuals (17.9 per cent of the respondents) indicated that they had founded at least one company. These individuals were then mailed a second survey that asked detailed questions about the formation of their firms. In this second round, 2111 founder surveys were completed, representing a response rate of 27.1 per cent.

4. Managing and developing the knowledge intensive entrepreneurship venture

4.1 INTRODUCTION

Managing a KIE venture involves internal and external processes, and relates to how and why management processes can help develop the ideas into a real company.

Managing is a type of 'doing', and this means that the manager and decision-makers need to think about a number of closely related topics that are discussed throughout this book:

- Opportunity exploration, conceptualization and exploitation.
- The use of internal and external resources.
- The dynamic nature of KIE ventures.

These topics are closely related to the fourth proposition of this book:

Significant differences exist between entrepreneurial management and general management. As one vital example, entrepreneurial management relies highly on the use of networks and emergence of access to resources. Therefore, management of KIE ventures requires a systemic understanding of processes and the relationship between individual and context in order to design and carry out this type of entrepreneurship.

The small firm often has constrained resources, and difficulties in hiring enough people or accessing enough finances to expand. Therefore, one example of differences is that entrepreneurial management greatly relies on the use of networks to access external resources like people or international markets.

Managing a KIE venture often involves tensions between what we may call 'exploration' and 'exploitation'. Therefore, going back to the classical distinction introduced by March (1991), one way of conceptualizing the problems facing the management of KIE ventures is the 'exploration' versus 'exploitation' trade-off. Exploration means trying out new directions while exploitation means developing for the market. Moreover, for KIE ventures, the literature suggests there are very specific and particular difficulties in balancing, on the one hand, the need to develop knowledge and ideas further and, on the other hand, to complete development work and then bring the products and services to market and users. These tensions can apply equally well to firms focused upon science and technology, as well as ones in creative industries.

This chapter focuses upon four variables that affect the processes of managing and developing KIE ventures in order to further develop these ideas.

As visualized in Figure 4.1, these aspects are: human resources; networks; growth patterns; and internationalization. They are four essential themes of managing that we have identified as of particular importance when learning about and engaging in KIE.

Figure 4.1   Development of KIE ventures

The first theme to be addressed is that of human resources, which can refer to people and their experience, and how to choose and motivate them. Although human resources management is also highly relevant to the management literature at large, it remains a particularly important issue for entrepreneurship due to the often small and new status of these ventures. There can also be a direct correlation to growth and survival, because if you don't hire the right people in a small organization, then the firm may fail by focusing upon the wrong activities or not delivering at the quality required.

The second theme deals with networks and these involve contacts and connections. They can be seen as an important way of managing relationships in order to access external resources and ideas. There are many different types of networks, so that the KIE venture has to consider who – academia, industry, investors or customers –why and what such relationships are to be used for (and at which stages). Literature on social capital and networks shows that these are important dimensions in order to understand the entrepreneurial process and, indeed, that social networking affects knowledge intensive firms' performance.

The third theme is related to growth, and although managing growth may seem straightforward, it is not. KIE ventures are often associated with high and rapid growth, which is why the management thereof is often challenging. Issues discussed in relation to growth patterns include emerging strategy, the shift from R&D to market (exploration versus exploitation) and learning in an entrepreneurial venture.

The fourth theme is internationalization. Previously, people thought that small companies first developed in their regional and national markets, and then started to think about international production and markets. Today, however, we know that many KIE ventures start with the global market as their target, and they may outsource all production from the beginning. Moreover, if they are science based, as in biotechnology, they may offer very specialized knowledge to buyers anywhere in the world. The organizational forms possible in the global world, as facilitated by trends like the web, IT and cheap transportation mean that KIE ventures are often international at the outset.

4.2 HUMAN RESOURCES

How to motivate and attract talent is a key issue as people are the most crucial aspect of knowledge, Individuals are also crucial in finding and developing ideas into innovations and products and services. One of the greatest challenges facing societies is the comparatively limited capacity to convert scientific breakthroughs, technological achievements and creative ideas into industrial and commercial successes.

The KIE venture needs talented people because the business is dependent upon them. The ability to utilize cutting-edge knowledge in innovative ways is time and time again highlighted as the single most important competence economies need to achieve in maintaining competitive advantage. Considering knowledge as a strategic asset matters in a world economy where manufacturing knowledge and capabilities are increasing not only being outsourced but also permanently displaced to low-cost countries.

There are many ways of accessing and using knowledge. Because of the connection between knowledge and innovation ability, many companies are trying to use and develop complex models for the transfer of different types of knowledge. For example, an innovation could involve inputs from firms, research institutes, inventors, entrepreneurs, universities and other sources. Moreover, in today's knowledge economy, a firm's ability to leverage knowledge in order to innovate is crucial.

Human resources are central to this debate, and especially in the way that knowledge is generated and exploited in the intersection between science and industrial application or between creativity and experience. This topic has been addressed in the management literature at large, but remains an issue of great interest to entrepreneurship, due to its direct correlation to growth and survival.

As with inputs, the role of the founder in new venture creation has been in focus, specifically on the characteristics of those individuals, such as leadership self-efficacy, perseverance, risk-taking ability and the role of transitions they experience during venture emergence (for example, Vecchio, 2003). The previous chapter discussed human resources issues in relation to how human resources are a determining input to the KIE process, especially types of personnel hired in the founding team in a KIE venture, the impact of prior experience and the challenges of taking on the differing roles as owner, founder or manager.

However, human resources mean more than this focus on the entrepreneur, founder or founding team. Seeing them as the only source of human capital is too limited to be useful in practice. It fails to recognize the important role of all the other employees in the new venture, and how those resources are configured to realize opportunities. As new firms grow through investments, through new ideas and through sales, they must also grow in the number of people they employ.

Human resources is a larger issue than the individual per se. This section therefore discusses how human resources are managed and utilized in KIE ventures in order to develop, conceptualize and exploit innovative opportunities. To this end, we discuss contemporary research results on the types of human competences involved in the creation of successful KIE ventures and in accessing external sources of knowledge.

4.2.1   Human Competencies

Traditional human resources topics concern recruiting, compensation and performance management, and these techniques all offer ways in which to pick the right people and make sure they deliver.

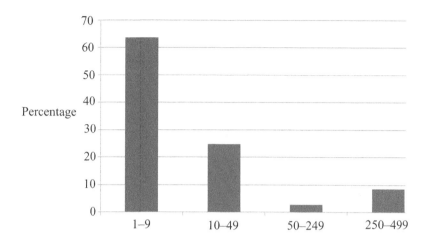

Figure 4.2   Size of KIE ventures

Figure 4.2 demonstrates the size of KIE ventures, based upon the AEGIS Survey (2012).

According to the AEGIS Survey (2012) of more than 4000 KIE ventures across Europe, the vast majority had less than nine employees, and as much as 85 per cent of all the responding KIE ventures had less than 50 employees.

This illustrates the extent and importance of considering the human resources aspects of such ventures very carefully in order to ensure their survival and contribution to the development of new knowledge-based innovation. Much of our knowledge about human resources concerns large firms, but some results will apply to small or emerging organizations.

KIE ventures face unique burdens during their initial stages, based on their youth or 'newness' and their small size. These two liabilities of being new and small present challenges for human resources management within these ventures as compared to large established organizations.

Young firms face the liabilities of newness, which may also include the challenges of entering unknown industries and markets. They must find ways to gain legitimacy in the sector and get customers to purchase, and to do so without the track record that experience and performance often provide to competitors (Stinchcombe, 1965; Hannan and Freeman, 1984). Moreover, small firms, regardless of age, face the liability of being small, and often lack the resources required to seek out new opportunities (Bruderl and Schussler, 1990; Ranger-Moore, 1997).

This leads us to expect certain trends for human resources in KIE ventures:

- Reduced reliance on formalized training of the human resources base.
- More informal employee management systems.
- Difficulty in recruiting due to lack of legitimacy or visibility.
- Difficulty in recruiting and retaining employees due to lack of financial resources.
- A reluctance to engage in costly human resources practices.
- A low number of formal human resources practices and professionals.

Taken together, these trends suggest that the venture could benefit from identifying a few of the human resources issues that they wish to address and decide how to solve them.

Hiring has been shown to be difficult: 25 per cent of small businesses view a lack of qualified workers as a threat not only to their plans to grow and expand, but more importantly as a threat to their very survival. So, there is a need to identify the main problem with human resources, and then find a reasonable solution. For example, there are different ways to solve the difficulty in recruiting as some firms are visible through their presence on targeted college campuses, while others may use their involvement in university-industry research centres to become more visible to MSc and PhD students. Many technology-based firms have given or sold stock shares to employees as a way of gaining loyalty and offering potential future rewards.

4.2.2 External Networks to Access Human Resources

External networks appear to be particularly important, as a way to access human resources. Moreover, in KIE ventures, these organizations need to possess the competences to acquire and implement external knowledge in order to foster the development of innovations and improve performance (Lichtenthaler and Lichtenthaler, 2009).

Hence, the combination of internal human resources and use of external networks are essential in order to ensure development of the product as well as the company itself. Selection of the human resources base is very important for small ventures (Hornsby and Kuratko, 1990) and may even be the key component of the overall effective management of a firm (Heneman and Berkley, 1999).

The firm needs its own internal resources in order to understand external developments. This applies in all three types of knowledge identified here, namely scientific, technological and creative knowledge; market knowledge; and business knowledge. It is not possible to out-source everything because in order to outsource activities, people in the firm need enough insight to be able to understand what is happening in the external environment.

Therefore, using the in-house human resources base in order to make a more efficient knowledge acquisition and inter-firm knowledge transfer relies on what is referred to as absorptive capacity. Absorptive capacity can be defined as the capability to identify, assimilate and apply external knowledge (Cohen and Levinthal, 1990; Zahra and George, 2002; Lichtenthaler and Lichtenthaler, 2009).

The AEGIS Survey (2012) underscores this point as it documents the extent to which KIE ventures rely on different knowledge sources for innovation. External knowledge sources are clearly the most important aspect, followed by the internal R&D competences.

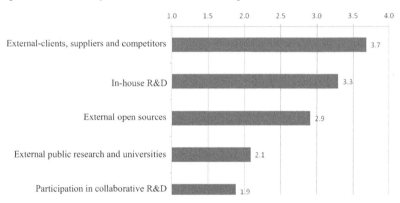

Figure 4.3   Sources of knowledge for KIE venture

Figure 4.3 shows the importance of external networks, and especially ones related to developments in the market, such as clients, suppliers and competitors.

Succeeding with these processes of using external networks to access human resources is not easy, however. Several studies have shown that organizations struggle with managing external knowledge acquisition, particularly during innovation development (Moenaert et al., 2000; Cassiman and Veugelers, 2006).

Moreover, in KIE ventures this capability is very clearly dependent on the abilities inside the firm. But since they often have a very limited human resources base, we can say that individuals in KIE ventures need four dimensions, namely identification, assimilation, transformation and exploitation. The KIE venture needs individuals who can operationalize absorptive capacity in the following ways:

- Identification refers to the behaviour of individuals reflecting the detection and acquisition of information that is new to their existing knowledge.
- Assimilation refers to the behaviour of individuals that represents the linking and comparison of new information to their existing knowledge, that is, the processing and understanding of information.
- Transformation refers to the behaviour of individuals by which they integrate new information into their own knowledge base and further extension of this knowledge.
- Exploitation is defined as the application of the new knowledge, for example, in a commercial setting, or the passing along and sharing of information to let others exploit and use the information.

All four dimensions can be considered as activities directed at the creation of the individual's knowledge base, which collectively form the foundation of the organizational ability to explore and exploit knowledge. Each dimension means that the employees need specific types of abilities, which go beyond education or experience per se. Moreover, these four dimensions are fundamentally different in scope and focus.

Therefore, under conditions of resource constraints, the KIE venture has to ask how they can ensure that all are covered. Here is one illustration.

> As a micro sized company the strategy was to exploit available external resources. In-house UECE5 focused on product development and communication activities. To overcome limited financial resources UECE5 took advantage of local manufacturing capacity and implemented a business model based on production outsourcing. Almost all UECE5's activities are outsourced ... This strategy allowed for the company to (almost) eliminate fixed costs, to gain production flexibility (responding easier to demand fluctuations) and for the company to concentrate on its core competencies (which in a broad sense are more commercial oriented activities). Moreover, the outsourcing strategy extended the internal knowledge base of the company. (UECE5 Inc.)

This example illustrates that even very small firms can successfully outsource as long as there is enough internal knowledge in the company to do so successfully.

The complexity of this issue of accessing human resources through external networks is discussed by, among others, Klofsten and Jones-Evans (2000), who focus on human competences involved in KIE. Their study focuses on academic entrepreneurship, which they define as all commercialization activities done by university employees and outside the normal university duties of basic research and teaching. They then examine the influence of gender, age, previous entrepreneurial experience, work experience and university environment on the entrepreneurship activities. The study focuses on Sweden and Ireland, which are often highlighted as particularly strong examples of academic entrepreneurship. Their results demonstrate that there is considerable entrepreneurial experience among academics in these countries, and that this translates into a high degree of involvement in 'soft' activities such as consultancy and contract research, but not into organizational creation via technology spin-offs. The researchers are thus diffusing their knowledge more widely in society, but they are not creating the academic spin-offs that we discussed in Chapter 2.

These results indicate important implications for managing human resources, in high-tech industries and ones dependent on universities. One aspect is that the competence or knowledge of how to orchestrate scientific knowledge in industrial settings is present in academic environments: and another way of conceptualizing this is that the scientific knowledge is applied only on an ad hoc basis, dependent upon the demands of the large established corporations rather than new venture creation.

Much evidence on knowledge management and absorptive capacity demonstrates that an ad hoc approach to knowledge application into new areas has a very limited and short-term effect. A reason could be that this approach to knowledge application only focuses on the dimensions of identification and direct exploitation of knowledge. This disregards the assimilation and transformation dimensions, which are essential in order for individuals to be able to successfully extend their own knowledge base and use it as a truly integrated part of developing the KIE venture.

This failure to include assimilation and transformation dimensions can also be illustrated by stating that science and technology are not developed far enough, in relation to the product and service, or what is known as the area of implementation. The rationale of scientific knowledge differs substantially from that of applied knowledge. For instance, Rindfleisch and Moorman (2001) examine the effect of acquisition of scientific technical information on organizations' new product development. The results of their study highlight that information redundancy between the exchanging partners has a negative effect on the acquisition of information.

One way of dealing with this complexity is to hire individuals with very different competencies. Having many employees with similar backgrounds may cause a focus on one issue rather than another issue, as illustrated here:

> The entrepreneurs hold respectively Master and PhD degrees with knowledge and experience within the Cube Sat. technology. Since the industry Space Inc. is involved in is extremely technological, the focus of Space Inc. is primarily technological. The education of the entrepreneurs and the subsequent PhDs are causes of great specialization within the technology development area that is not easily transferred to managerial competences. Thus, in the early years of Space Inc. the focus on sales and business development was limited. This is not necessarily a deliberate choice, but rather a natural consequence, reflected by the backgrounds and experiences of the founders. Since its conception Space Inc. has been forced to move from being a company with a strong technological focus to a company capable of both developing and commercializing on its products. (AAU, Space Inc.)

As another example, in the biotechnology industry, one of the first and best known companies is Genentech. Genentech hired postdoc researchers trained with top scientists – who entered the board but remained working at their university, University of California at San Fransisco (UCSF). However, they also quickly hired individuals with long industrial experience in related industries (McKelvey, 1996).

4.2.3   Summary about Human Resources

Managing the competences of the human resources base is indeed a challenge in KIE ventures. The challenges arise due to the limited number of employees, and who must be able to perform multiple roles during growth periods in the venture. Managers need to find or train employees who have the ability to perform multiple, demanding roles. This can be difficult to achieve, however, because these roles may require an understanding of very different types of knowledge. Some issues are that it can be very difficult for the individual to switch between fields of knowledge, and that some individuals are generalists while others are specialists.

Key take-away points from the discussions include:

- The particularities of KIE ventures in terms of how young and small they are in combination with high demands in terms of knowledge assets pose high demands on the human resources base. Such demands include:

    - The ability to fulfil more than one role.
    - Complementary mixing of technical and managerial competences.
    - The ability of each employee to be highly self-driven and self-managed.
    - The ability of each employee to continuously self-evaluate the relevance and priority of tasks.
    - The need for networking.

Being able to access human resources and knowledge through external networks is key to being able to engage in the processes of opportunity exploration, conceptualization and exploitation. Because the development of the firm through a combination of individuals and opportunities represents an ongoing and dynamic process, this also requires that the people – or the human resources base – need a high degree of absorptive capacity. For them, absorptive capacity is related not only to the intake of new knowledge for further development, but also to the absorption of external knowledge and competences that will advance the ability to exploit the product, service and market of the KIE venture.

The distinction between internal and external resources is often not so useful to make in the sense that the employees of KIE ventures rely heavily on external networks of various types in order to achieve growth.

4.2.4 Questions for Discussion

1. How does the liability of being small and young affect the human resources in KIE ventures?
2. Which human resources measures could be taken to overcome the liability of being small and young?
3. Which human resources competences are needed in KIE ventures?
4. Can you find examples for the four types of absorptive capacity in relation to a specific case firm?

4.3 NETWORKS

Networks are important topics in relation to KIE, and they have been introduced above when discussing human resources. The evidence suggests that the process of managing KIE ventures is strongly affected by the network activities of the venture. Moreover, in 1986, Aldrich and Zimmer argued that the entrepreneur is embedded in a social network, which plays a critical role in the entrepreneurial process. This helps access to resources and ideas, as discussed in Chapter 3, but also impacts the management and development of the KIE venture.

Thus, as a definition, social networks are composed of a set of actors (individuals or organizations) and a set of linkages between the actors (Brass, 1992). These actors and linkages have been found to influence the firm. Important issues that can be examined include ones such as how networks affect the entrepreneurial teams; whether networks represent formal or informal relationships; the types of partners in these relationships such as academia, industry, investors or customers; the motivations for networks; and the actual stage of development for the KIE venture.

Networks are important concepts and part of the management process in entrepreneurial processes. Moreover, networks affect performance, but exactly how and why do they do this?

The literature review that was done as a foundation for this book shows that three aspects of networks are critical to managing KIE ventures:

1. The nature of the content that is exchanged between actors.
2. Governance mechanisms.
3. Network structure as created by the linkages and relationships between actors.

These help explain how and why networks affect the recognition and realization of innovative opportunities as well as their impact on performance.

4.3.1 Content and Purpose of Networks

The first question to ask is about the content and purpose of networks, as compared to the ambitions of the firms in terms of how to access knowledge and resources.

Networks mean that there are actors and linkages. Interpersonal and interorganizational relationships provide a structure, through which actors gain access to a variety of resources held by other actors. Some work exists on the role of networks to access capital (for example, Bates, 1997), as illustrated under 'Financing' in Chapter 3. Yet most research has addressed the entrepreneur's access to intangible resources.

One key benefit of networks for the entrepreneurial process is the access they provide to information and advice. Ties to venture capitalists and professional service organizations, for example, are a means for tapping into key talent and market information (Freeman, 1999). A number of studies document that entrepreneurs consistently use networks to get ideas and gather information to recognize entrepreneurial opportunities (Smeltzer et al., 1991; Singh et al., 1999; Hoang and Young, 2000).

Thus, networks can be used for learning about entrepreneurship and obtaining advice and help in spotting opportunities, as shown below.

> The firm's most important relationships are those with its customers. These relationships and its internal resources are the most important resources in product development. Relationships with suppliers and research institutes play a minor role as well. The knowledge gained as a result of these relationships relates most importantly to finding new customers; other important areas include information about the competition and tax and legal advice. To some extent the relationships are also useful for product development, operations management and finding new distribution channel. (Softrise Inc.)

This illustration shows that the content of information distributed through a network may range over many different areas.

Social capital is another concept, and sometimes it is used to describe the benefits of networks, although many different definitions exist. Let us examine one study. Groen et al. (2008) suggest that entrepreneurs use four types of functions to develop their business: namely

- goal attainment => strategic capital
- pattern maintenance => cultural capital
- social networking => social capital
- economic optimization => economic capital.

They argue that building sustainable firms requires the development of all four functions. The firm must develop these functions internally, and to do so they also need to develop four types of capital in relation to external partners, which correspond to strategic, cultural, economic and social. KIE ventures require all four types of capital to build a sustainable position in the long term, yet in the short term a start-up may use its social capital to counterbalance a complete lack of economic capital. This suggests that social capital helps access financing, and other resources to tide them over.

However, the reliance on networks is not constrained to the start-up stage. Entrepreneurs continue to rely on networks during later phases for business information, advice and problem solving, with some contacts providing multiple resources (Johannisson et al., 1994). Ties to distributors, suppliers, competitors or customer organizations can be important as conduits of information and know-how (Brown and Butler, 1995). These types of networks help provide information in particular about market knowledge, such as customers' preferences.

Results from the AEGIS Survey (2012) show that the networking activities of KIE ventures are very diverse.

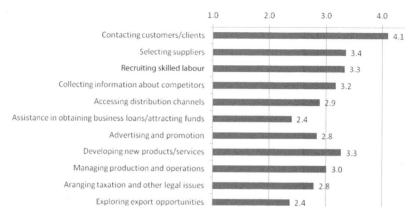

Figure 4.4   Why KIE ventures use networks

Figure 4.4 demonstrates how networks aid the development of the venture in several aspects, ranging from the obvious aspects, such as contacting customers and clients, to the less obvious, such as managing production and operations.

Another aspect of the value of networks to small firms has to do with the intangible impacts, which can affect the later development and performance of the firm. Many discussions focus on networks in terms of exchange of information, advice and emotional support, but relationships can also have more indirect benefits in terms of reputational or signalling content (Deeds et al., 1997; Stuart et al., 1999; Higgins and Gulati, 2000; Shane and Cable, 2002).

Moreover, in the uncertain and dynamic conditions under which most KIE activity occurs, potential investors and employees are likely to seek information and signals that provide information about the underlying potential of the KIE venture that they wish to evaluate. Entrepreneurs seek legitimacy to reduce this perceived risk by associating with or gaining explicit certification from well-regarded individuals and organizations. Positive perceptions that are based on a firm's network ties may in turn lead to subsequent beneficial resource exchanges for both partners.

4.3.2 Governance of Networks

Other questions are how networks are governed, and how the KIE venture should behave in order to function well in a network.

Networks are generally seen as an alternative governance form to markets. Governance as a concept has to do with how things are decided and distributed among actors, with goal attainment for the overall system, and the effects upon the linkages developed. Therefore, within networks, distinctive governance mechanisms can be identified and discussed in terms of coordinating the network exchanges.

Scholars have defined network governance as the reliance on 'implicit and open-ended contracts' that are supported by social mechanisms, such as power and influence (Brass, 1984; Thorelli, 1986; Krackhardt, 1990) as well as the threat of exclusion and loss of reputation (Portes and Sensebrenner, 1993; Jones et al., 1997), rather than any legal implications.

Networks thus include many social organizational forms. Trust, for example, may be key to working with other organizations as shown below.

> In order to be of interest for the large customers we often have to exaggerate how far we are in the process of maturing the product. It's OK to say that we expect the market potential to be X without being 100% sure. But, you can't say that you know for sure unless you are absolutely sure, which is very rare at this stage of understanding the potential of our technology. You must never ever lie – about the capabilities of your product, about your ability to deliver or anything else. If you are caught in a lie even once, you have lost the trust of your customer or potential investor. Nobody will play with you if you gain a reputation of not being trustworthy. So even one lie can kill off a small company like ours. (Sensor Inc.)

So there are also long-term effects of how an actor behaves within a network. Trust between partners is often cited as a critical element of network exchange, and also seen, in turn, to enhance the quality of the resource flows (Larson, 1992; Lorenzoni and Lipparini, 1999; Jacobsen and Lassen, 2012). The above illustration shows that trust and networks are particularly important to the small firms as they have little other reputation or branding to fall back upon.

Mutual trust as a governance mechanism is based on the belief in the other partner's reliability in terms of fulfillment of obligation in an exchange (Pruitt, 1981). Trust allows both parties to assume that each will take actions that are foreseeable and mutually acceptable (Powell, 1990; Das and Teng, 1998). A number of scholars have asserted that these distinctive elements of network governance can be particularly important to KIE ventures to create cost advantages in comparison to coordination through market or bureaucratic mechanisms (Thorelli, 1986; Jarillo, 1988; Starr and Macmillan, 1990; Jones et al., 1997). Trust also affects the depth and fullness of exchange relations in the linkages, and this means that trust will especially affect the exchange of information (Saxenian, 1991; Lorenzoni and Lipparini, 1999; Hite, 2000).

Bagchi-Sen (2007), for example, examines the importance of alliances as an innovation strategy by KIE ventures. They show that university collaborations are critical for enhancing credibility and reputation in the scientific and business community, while interfirm collaborations are critical for product development and commercialization. Alliances with foreign firms are critically important for entering foreign markets and these markets are as important as the domestic market in supporting the revenue base of biotechnology firms.

Thus, the different types of networks will provide different types of information, which correspond to our three types of scientific, technological and creative; market; and business knowledge.

4.3.3 Structure of Networks

A third question to consider when managing a KIE venture is how the firm relates to the overall structure of the network. A defining characteristic of a network is that the actors and linkages will in turn affect the dynamics of social structures between the KIE venture and external environment. Network structure is defined as the pattern of direct and indirect ties between actors.

A general assumption made in theories dealing with social networks is that actors' positioning within a network structure has an important impact on resource flows. Therefore, in our case, positioning in the network would have an impact on entrepreneurial outcomes and performance. What matters then is not the actors per se but their position in the network structure and their ability to use this network.

A variety of empirical measures has been developed and utilized to understand patterns within a social network structure, and these are collectively known as social network analysis, with software packages available. Readers can access these software tools and use them to analyse specific companies. These measures can also be used to characterize the positions of entrepreneurs as individuals, or the KIE ventures, in the network.

One important measure is the size of a network, defined as the number of direct links between a focal actor and other actors. Analyses of network size measure the extent to which resources can be accessed by the individual entrepreneur (Aldrich and Reese, 1993; Hansen, 1995) as well as at the level of the organization (Katila, 1997; Freeman, 1999; Katila and Mang, 1999; Baum et al., 2000).

Another measure of network position is centrality. This measures the centrality of ties to others relative to the whole network structure. This measure explicitly includes the idea that high centrality leads to the ability to access (or control) resources through indirect as well as direct links. Degree of centrality addresses the ability of actors to access other actors in their network, which one could also relate back to our discussion on the absorptive capacity of the employees in the KIE venture.

Network size and centrality measure the amount of resources an actor can access, but other patterns in the network structure also influence their access to a diversity of resources. Diversity of knowledge is one of the central discussions when trying to understand the relationship between knowledge, innovation and entrepreneurship.

This need for diverse types of content through a changing network structure is illustrated in the following:

> The case of Micropos nicely illustrates how a small medtech start-up company needs to develop relationships to a broad range of external actors in order to grow beyond the initial stages. The incubator as well as several public financing organizations (regional as well as national) played a crucial role before and after the company was formed (2003). Now, eight years later, some of these relationships remain but are no longer directly central for the company's development. The most important and challenging direct task for a start-up company is to build relationships to potential users and customers. The links to academia however continue to serve an important indirect role as a quality reference for customers. (Micropos)

Diversity of types of networks matters over time to this company, and while initially regional financing and universities played a key role, later the networks to potential users and customers were more important.

The manager of a KIE venture also faces an inherent trade-off between depth of knowledge and diversity of knowledge that one can access through networks. Granovetter's (1973) notion of weak ties, in particular, describes the extent to which actors are able to gain access to new information and ideas through ties that lie outside their immediate contacts.

Capaldo (2007) investigates whether, why and how different network architectures exert asymmetric impacts on the innovative capability of the network's leading actor. His findings show that the ability to integrate a large periphery of heterogeneous weak ties and a core of strong ties constitutes the lead firm's relational capability. This provides fertile ground for leading firms in knowledge intensive networks to gain competitive advantages, whose sustainability is primarily based on the dynamic innovative capability resulting from leveraging dual network architecture.

Complementary to the benefits of weak ties is the concept of structural holes, defined as the absence of ties between actors. There are theorized benefits of bridging structural holes. Occupying a bridging position provides an opportunity to influence those who are otherwise unconnected to the broader network (Krackhardt, 1995). Given this opportunity for diverse contacts, spanning structural holes can, for example, increase the central actor's exposure to novel information. This in turn may spur learning and the development of internal capabilities that ultimately enhance performance (McEvily and Zaheer, 1999; Baum et al., 2000).

Moreover, in relation to KIE, the structure of the network will likely influence the KIE ventures by providing information that affects how the founder and firm will be able to identify and act upon the notion of opportunity. This helps develop market opportunities, which are designed and exploited through the KIE venture.

De Carolis et al. (2009) tested the effects of the interplay of social capital and cognition on a sample of 269 entrepreneurs, and their results confirm that social networks and relational capital enhance levels of the illusion of control, which is directly related to the progress of new venture creation. Their research suggests that social capital is not enough; and that the type of person involved in network relationships matters to new venture creation.

Specifically, they proposed that the benefits of social networks and the relational capital contained within those networks indirectly impact new venture creation through cognitive bias, and especially the illusion of control and risk propensity. This suggests that entrepreneurs use networks in ways that also enhance the conception of the business environment, in ways that augment the individual characteristics and traits, as discussed in Chapter 3.

4.3.4 Summary about Networks

Networks influence KIE ventures through aspects like content, governance and the overall network structure. Key take-aways from the discussions include the following.

As KIE ventures are by definition formed under the premise of serious resource constraint, networks often become important sources of knowledge, resources and support, which the KIE venture cannot achieve by other means. Networks include actors and linkages.

The influence of networks and networking on KIE involves several aspects:

- The network content includes different types of knowledge and recognition of opportunities that can be transferred through the network. It refers to the reasons the KIE venture has for participating in the network.
- A variety of different networks exist, which could provide the venture with benefits such as specific goal attainment, pattern maintenance, social networking and economic optimization.
- The KIE venture's ability to make use of networks is influenced by the structure of the particular network in terms of the size of the network (how many resources are available in the network), the centrality of the position of the KIE venture within the network (how accessible are the resources in the network) and the diversity of resources (how different are the resources of the network).

The governance of networks is composed of ties that may be both formal and informal. Formal ties are related to contract relationships whereas informal ties often rely upon trust. Trust between the different actors means a belief in the other partner's reliability in fulfilling obligation. Trust, in turn, allows both parties to assume that each will take actions that are foreseeable and mutually acceptable, and this is probably the most important mechanism governing these networks.

4.3.5 Questions for Discussion

1. Explain in your own words why networks are highly important to KIE venture development.
2. What are the central elements that the manager should consider when utilizing networks?

3.   What are the advantages, and potential problems, of working through networks?

4.4 GROWTH

Managing KIE ventures leads to specific challenges in relation to growth. Growth is not easy. Managing a fast-growing venture can be quite turbulent with ups and down, and so errors of judgement about the firm or its environment can easily lead to failures, which in turn cause performance problems in the long run.

Indeed, growth in KIE ventures is associated with many difficulties and strains upon the organization, and it is not easy to continuously reorganize in the way suggested in this section. The issues discussed below have been most commonly studied in R&D intensive firms and high-tech sectors. Our view is that these challenges can be found in firms in services, high-tech sectors as well as in low-tech sectors. Many specific challenges relate to the nature of growth, which is related to the liability of being new and of small size. Growth is often uneven, with major shifts towards expansion or contraction common. This type of change can occur at a high pace. There are also questions about how to manage the overall foci of the company, in that many, but not all of these challenges have to do with a more concentrated focus upon market and business knowledge as valuable to the firm.

4.4.1 Continuous Reorganizing

A small firm needs to reorganize its resources over time, and this is often a continuous process. The firm thereby needs to develop strategies that are adjusted to the external environment or ecosystem. The KIE venture should have an 'emergent' strategy, which means the strategic goals developed during the business development process. This ability to continuously organize and reorganize can be related to the concepts of emergence and effectuation, which are often discussed as particular to entrepreneurship (Sarasvathy, 2001). Our view is that the KIE venture must be proactive in building organizational structure, and in understanding the external environment. By so doing, it will be able to help design innovative opportunities and develop internal capabilities to manage a volatile environment with high levels of uncertainty.

One thing to consider is that the management practices will often differ between large and small firms. There are several aspects that set the management of KIE ventures apart from strategic management in larger organizations. One major aspect is the fact that in larger organizations competitive advantage is often created deliberately as a result of the pursuit of explicit policies and procedures. Consequently, strategic management has become a predictive process (Faulkner and Johnson, 1992). Thus, in contrast, competitive advantage in small firms often arises emergently as a result of particular operating circumstances surrounding the enterprise, tied to how the individuals and team inside the firm can interpret and react to the external changes.

Moreover, in KIE ventures, the strategic management becomes primarily an adaptive and reflective process concerned with manipulating a limited amount of resources. As such, the efforts are not concentrated on predicting or controlling the operating environment, but on adapting as quickly as possible to the changing demands of this environment (Jennings and Beaver, 1997).

This management process is often characterized by the decisions reflecting the highly personalized preferences and capabilities of the owner, manager and key staff. One can say that the organizational strategy often develops as a consequence of the external environment, with the interplay of a few key human resources. An alternative mode of organizing is the self-organizing and decentralized decision-making model.

To better define the options for management in these circumstances, Nicholls-Nixon (2005) outlines five practices. These are built on the concept of self-organizing, and are designed to help firms cope with the continuous and unpredictable change that characterizes daily life in a fast-growing enterprise. They are:

- Developing a clear sense of the firm's business logic to guide individual actions and interactions when formal structures and systems are inadequate.
- Creating systems that capture meaningful information for tracking firm performance and providing opportunities (formal and informal) to share and interpret this information within the organization, so that employees have a basis for creative problem solving when unpredictable situations emerge.
- Emphasizing relationship building, both within the firm and with external stakeholders such as customers and suppliers, so that people can access needed expertise and resources to address problems and opportunities as they arise.
- Minimizing the potential for disruptive organizational politics in order to sustain the voluntary and cooperative interactions that form the basis for self-organizing behaviour.

- Adopting a leadership style that focuses more on facilitating than directing or controlling the process of growth, so that the organization can respond to changing conditions in real time.

These management practices suggest that self-organization can be developed into a core capability, and that this is especially relevant in KIE ventures dealing with high growth rates or volatile growth. Managers can take a series of conscious decisions and actions to develop the organizational structures of these five practices that support self-organizing behaviour. In other words, this implies that management is not just a random process of reacting to change, but that managers of high-growth firms can build this capability.

The following provides an illustration of the continuous change facing this type of venture, and therefore why the manager may need to build structures to help support self-organizing behaviour.

> Yes, we have developed a sensor technology capable of the most extraordinary things. But, in order for our company to be a success, we also continuously need to take a lot of steps backwards, in order to demonstrate what the technology cannot do (quality tests) or how to rethink how our organizational set-up should be in order to best take advantage of the technology. This is a real challenge, as the great interest for most of us is to develop the technology. But, we have been forced to realize that in order to be attractive for investors and customers these are necessary steps to take every time the technology insights change even the slightest bit. For instance, we have changed primary market focus a number of times in steps with our increased knowledge of the strengths and weaknesses of the technology as well as our (market) awareness has been raised with customers and investors. The advantages of being as small as we are, is that we are able to make these changes as soon as we become aware of the need to do so. We don't have a lot of resources tied up in only one approach or one system. (Sensor Inc.)

This case shows how this company changed over time. A key necessity is to try to respond, often requiring changes in understanding the potential products and services that could be developed, based upon the underlying resources and ideas.

But this could also have some implications for organizational structure, and also further develop the human resources issues already addressed in this chapter.

This self-organizing approach has the distinct advantage of being adaptive, fast responding and closely related to the contemporary developments on the market. Management is seen as 'emergent' because decisions come as circumstances change, rather than based on a top-down development plan. Naturally, in many situations, one person – usually the founder or entrepreneur cum manager – makes most decisions.

Among others, Lichtenstein et al. (2006) show how the management competences of a KIE venture revolves around the ability to continuously reorganize. They analyse three modes of organizing: vision, strategic organizing and tactical organizing. Using longitudinal analysis they find a nearly simultaneous shift in all three modes in successful KIEs. They define this as an 'emergence event', and provide a process model of organizational emergence showing that a shift in tactical organizing generates a shift in strategic organizing, which results in a shift in the vision (identity) of the firm.

Therefore, for the emergent management practice to work, an essential element is the balance between strategic goals and business plans with the need to delegate decision-making and support the autonomy of individuals. Autonomy refers to the independent actions of an individual or a team in bringing forth an idea or a vision and carrying it through to completion, and as such, their actions are taken free of rigid restrictions imposed from the top. The key idea is that the individual or team will be able to act independently, make key decisions and proceed to implement decisions. Such delegation of decision-making and autonomy is assumed to give them the freedom to explore new options. This, in turn, should be supported by a structure, where employees and management can jointly evaluate what to do and how to accomplish the tasks, and that also generates a sense of control over one's own work and ideas.

This management ideal is based on the idea to guide and assist rather than interfere with and control the innovators. This means that a key – but challenging – task for managers is to decide how to organize resources and processes in such a way as to transition the KIE venture from a focus upon ideas, through the initial stage and into a profitable and growth-oriented stage.

However, the reader should also be aware that this type of emergent strategy is very vulnerable to discontinuity of management and key staff. In particular, if they leave or if venture capital brings in a new manager then the whole direction of the company can change. If the manager makes a bad choice, then the whole venture can be exposed to serious problems, given the liability of being new and small.

4.4.2 Transitioning from R&D and Creativity to the Market

One of the topics often highlighted in entrepreneurship literature and innovation management literature alike is related to the difficulties experienced by many firms in creating balance between R&D activities and activities focusing on bringing products efficiently to market.

This is often thought of as a balance between exploration (of new areas) and exploitation (or realization of existing areas), which is a classical distinction introduced by March (1991). Search processes – or exploration processes – can be organized in many different ways, and in most KIE ventures, R&D and skilled employees play a very significant role, and that holds for firms in low-tech and traditional sectors as well as in high-tech sectors. They need to move the developments from the labs and R&D departments into products and services for the market place. Moreover, their investment into R&D and creative expressions leads to new technologies and state-of-the-art knowledge, which is highly relevant for the ability to innovate.

While a general problem for innovation and entrepreneurship, the emphasis here is on how these knowledge intensive ventures and industries can deal with such challenges. The existing literature focuses upon R&D intensive firms such as ones found in high-tech sectors or as academic spin-offs. The underlying reasoning about the need to shift focus upon the most relevant type of knowledge for the firm can also be applied to low-tech sectors and services. Within the creative industries and service industries, for example, there will be a similar need to balance managerial tasks for business knowledge with the ones wishing to further develop the service ideas and creative expressions.

As an early example, Berry (1996) discusses the management phenomenon underlying corporate transformation processes in small high-tech firms. He argues that firms are unlikely to achieve corporate transformation unless the managers adopt a strategic approach to managing the business and technology development. This is related to the impact of the founder and human resources issues. Significantly, firms that fail to evolve towards a market-led organization and a strategic orientation are the same ones where management is dominated by individuals concerned with science and technology. He further concludes that the critical determinant of the firm's viability and achievements in the long term is the strategic awareness of the technical entrepreneur. This means that the scientific and technical experts tend to focus upon further exploration, but they can also develop a strategic orientation to focus upon exploitation and commercialization.

A key issue to consider is that the advancement of scientific, technological and creative knowledge does not guarantee commercial success and diffusion on the market. As a matter of fact, the more sophisticated the R&D and creative processes become, the more complex, difficult and uncertain is the path from ideas to the market place. Many entrepreneurs who have gone through this process mention that transitioning from R&D

and creativity to production, service provision and market ramp-up is as difficult as the development of the ideas themselves.

In March's (1991) work, the conflict between exploration and exploitation is related to managing the organizational structure. Both exploration and exploitation processes are greatly required in these ventures, but they have fundamentally different objectives, which require very different mindsets and organizational set-ups. But why is it difficult? Key difficulties of transitioning from ideas to market involve the existing configuration of resources, such as human resources, the equipment and the organizational structures that favour research but are often diametrically opposite to those required for efficient production.

Let us think of the specific case of R&D intensive firms, which have key technologies and production. On the one hand R&D in KIE ventures typically favours agility, free-thinking academics and small, tightly knitted groups, but on the other hand manufacturing production tends to require a disciplined workforce, clearly described tasks and job design, and production equipment, which have very different requirements than testing equipment. If the technology leads to large-scale manufacturing, then there is often a need for the firm to transform to a focus on production, that is, once the technology is mature enough and ready for production. As we discussed previously, this is the stage where most investments by venture capital and other formal types of financing occur as well as corporate capital investments, as the firm begins to sell products and services.

The difficulties of balancing exploration and exploitation may not apply to all firms, though, as it should be noted that some KIE ventures will instead outsource production, and this has become increasingly possible in the global world, and is facilitated by the web. However, they will still need similar absorbable capabilities to organize and lead the structured production processes. Other firms deliver services, and scaling up services is at least as challenging as scaling up production.

There is an evolution from opportunity-driven to resource-driven management. The focus for success shifts as the enterprise evolves, from sensing and seizing opportunity to realizing those opportunities, which is seen as resource-driven management and more similar to how the large organizations are managed. They begin to concentrate more on having products and services for sale, and on protecting and utilizing the resources that have been acquired.

Thus, in making this shift to resource-driven management, the ways of working must change. This shift – as well as learning how to work in a more structured decision-making organization – can lead to problems. For example, Sykes and Block (1989) discuss how the transition from being exploration oriented to being exploitation oriented also creates a fundamental conflict between the management requirements of running a new venture or a mature company. The manager needs to be aware of these conflicts, and also address them explicitly, in step with the growth of the KIE venture towards a more mature organization. The five management practices outlined at the beginning of this section suggest that the growing venture can still maintain flexibility and adaptability, even as structures become more formalized and rigid.

Perhaps one of the major challenges in this adaptation to new requirements from the external environment is the ability to invent and tolerate a mix of apparently contradictory policies and practices. This is a very difficult process, which poses a number of problems or barriers to the KIE venture. Feldman and Klofsten (2000) explore barriers to growth in key areas that can become increasingly problematic for some KIE ventures as they grow and evolve from their early status as small-scale ventures.

These potential growth barriers can occur in finance, competition from new firms or products and organizational integration of resources. The authors argue that KIE ventures can encounter the same problems associated with poor communication, bureaucracy and loss of entre- preneurial spirit that plague large firms. They also show that the routines used to promote growth based on collaboration can sometimes create problems for firms as they ignore new challenges. The worse case is that the firm ends up with the disadvantages of management practices from both small and large firms, and the best one is that the firm can accept is a mix of managerial decisions and actions that draw from the managerial practices of both large and small firms to continue to both explore and exploit.

We propose that managers of KIE ventures need to be aware and explicitly develop routines for the evolution from opportunity-driven to resource-driven management. They also need to be aware of two possible barriers to growth.

First, there is the destructive conflict between the establishment of formal needs and policies of the maturing firm and the continued needs for exploration of the venture. Second, there is the misdirection of new ventures into an unsuccessful direction because of the imposition of irrelevant and often damaging practices based upon a more structured corporate management approach.

To innovate successfully the maturing KIE venture must overcome these barriers. One way to do so is to follow pluralistic management practices adapted to the needs of incorporating exploration as well as exploitation in the maturing venture. This means that different parts of the firm may be managed differently in terms of goals and assessment practices, and in order to highlight the need to both innovate and use existing resources as efficiently as possible. Implementing both in the same small firm will require flexibility, responsiveness, and resourcefulness.

4.4.3 Summary about Growth

This section looked at the challenges that managers of KIE must address. The key conflicts are between exploration and exploitation, and how to develop a relevant mix of managerial processes and ideas and to incorporate both of them inside the same firm.

Several factors influence KIE management and imply that this type of management differs significantly from that of larger and more mature organizations:

- Growth patterns. KIE ventures often follow very discontinuous patterns of growth, pendular between periods of little organizational growth, but high focus on technology development, and periods of rapid organizational growth and less focus on technological development.
- Such discontinuity in focus also requires a management approach that can embrace very different requirements in terms of focus, structures, prioritization of task, resource allocation, human resources demands, training of staff and so on.
- Speed of growth. The speed of growth – but also the potential speed of contraction of the KIE venture – pose specific challenges for KIE management.
- As we have seen throughout this section, this may entail a destructive conflict between the rapid establishment of formal needs and policies of the maturing firm and the continued need for exploration of the venture. As such, the management practices need to be able to address pluralistic needs simultaneously.

The understanding of KIE as a dynamic system also suggests that one should first evaluate performance over a much longer time than usually assumed – and examine both ups and downs – but also consider learning as a means of addressing these management challenges.

4.4.4 Questions for Discussion

1. How do potential barriers to growth emerge in the areas of finance, organizational integration, competition and product development and collaboration?
2. How do these barriers emerge over time as smaller ventures become larger and older?
3. Discuss which elements managers of KIE ventures need to consider continuously in order to create the best fit between exploration and exploitation.

4.5 INTERNATIONALIZATION

Internationalization is of particular interest to KIE ventures given that the knowledge and innovative opportunities created often have global potential, and they are not restricted to regional or national boundaries. This means that internationalization may be a core feature, running from accessing resources and ideas, through management and to performance.

Moreover, in an international knowledge economy, KIE serves as a key mechanism for societies and economies, by which knowledge created in one organization becomes commercialized in a new venture, and likewise, how knowledge created in one country is developed or applied in another. Hence, managing KIE ventures also implies thinking about the global world. There is a need to analyse how to access knowledge and how to organize and set up the venture across multiple national boundaries, as well as developing international markets.

4.5.1 Differences between Large and Small Organizations

Managing internationalization in this context probably bears little resemblance to international management processes in larger firms. Large R&D intensive firms often have multiple R&D centres and many years of experience. As with the general management processes discussed above, managing international processes in KIE ventures tends to differ – and for similar reasons related to the liabilities of newness and small size.

The main reason why it differs is that many KIE ventures have distinct disadvantages, especially in the start-up phase:

- lack of existing networks
- lack of existing market knowledge
- lack of resources to invest in and carry out high risk projects

- lack of experience on how to best develop and exploit new opportunities
- generally, a lack of personnel with international business experience.

These firms may have great ideas, but face obstacles in internationalization. They may also lack depth in all three types of knowledge, namely scientific, technological and creative, market and business. However, the KIE venture can overcome many of these disadvantages through, for example, sharing risks through global financial instruments or relying upon international professional networks of the entrepreneur and founder.

Succeeding in the global market requires the same attributes as entrepreneurship in general, namely innovativeness, risk-taking and entrepreneurial orientation. Moving to the international stage does place additional demands compared to developing the local market. New ventures that reach the global market quickly after they are started are driven by a set of internal and external forces to do so, as elucidated below.

The reason they become international can sometimes be linked to managers and owners, and their experiences. Bell et al. (2004) explore the linkages between the overall business strategies of small firms and their patterns, processes and pace of internationalization. Their findings suggest that business policies matter, and especially those linked to ownership and changes in management. New owners and managers can influence how international the firm becomes, as well as the geographical areas into which they expand. There are similarly close relationships between the product policies and the market focus in that new product or process innovation often provide an important stimulus to international expansion of the market. There may be limited markets in the close geographical area, or customers may be found abroad.

This is related to one particularly interesting finding, namely that systematic differences exist in the patterns, processes and pace of internationalization between KIE firms within manufacturing compared to other small firms within traditional manufacturing. Many KIE firms have an international orientation from inception. They have a new product development process focusing upon the requirements of international markets; tend to gravitate towards lead markets in the particular industry sector globally; a planned and structured approach to overseas markets; rapid internationalization; and more variety in market servicing modes.

Generally, the reasons for going abroad have to do with markets, as well as niche products. The international KIE ventures pursue market-based strategies, seeking broad market coverage through developing numerous distribution channels, serving numerous customers in diverse geographic markets and developing high market or product visibility. They will often use agents and sales offices abroad. In terms of product strategy, the evidence suggests that international KIE ventures typically follow a niche strategy (for example, Knight et al., 2004; Crick, 2009).

Possibly, these firms differ in the scale at which they become global. It has also been argued that the international ventures emphasize a more aggressive entry strategy to foreign markets, by building on outside financial and production resources to enter numerous geographical markets on a large scale (Chetty and Wilson, 2003; Coviello, 2006). Securing patent technology may also be an important component of their strategy (Fan and Phan, 2007). This suggests that the international ventures compete by entering their niche on a large scale, seeking to penetrate multiple geographic markets, with the recognition that external resources are necessary to support such an entry.

All in all, internationalization can be a key feature, despite the initial disadvantages and these firms may indeed have a strong rationale to develop an understanding of the international arena from the beginning. Many KIE ventures are born global, which means that they start their business with internationalization in mind from the beginning (see, for example, McDougall and Oviatt, 2000). This suggests that internationalization processes in the context of KIE differ significantly from more traditional businesses that become international later on after they have accumulated resources and competencies to go global.

4.5.2   Model for Thinking about Internationalization

In order to understand the internationalization process of KIE ventures, the following model, proposed in Lassen et al. (2012), specifies the aspects to take into consideration. The model illustrates the dynamic relationship between internal and external factors of the KIE venture, when they move to internationalization. The model particularly highlights how these factors influence the speed to market, entry mode decisions, geographical representation, coordination of supply chain activities and product strategies applied by KIE ventures.

Often, the speed to market can be defined as first international sales. However, this may not be an appropriate measure of the KIE ventures'

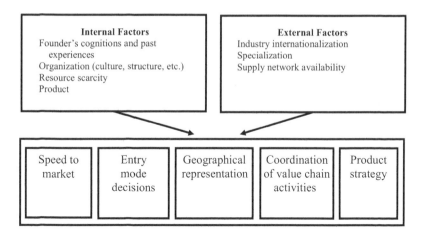

Figure 4.5   Factors in KIE internationalization

degree of internationalization as sales often occur somewhat later in the maturity development of the KIE.

Rather, their initial presence on international markets is often driven by knowledge exploration and collaboration with other companies with similar or compatible knowledge. This approach reflects their need to gradually build up a new market, rather than focus on penetrating an existing market.

> As a micro sized company, the strategy was to exploit available external resources ... In–house, UECE5 focused on product development and communication activities. To overcome limited financial resources, UECE5 took advantage of local manufacturing capacity and implemented a business model based on production outsourcing, almost all UECE5's activities are outsourced ... This strategy allowed for the company to (almost) eliminate fixed costs, to gain production flexibility (responding easier to demand fluctuations) and for the company to concentrate on its core competencies (which in a broad sense are more commercial oriented activities). Moreover, the outsourcing strategy extended the internal knowledge base of the company. (UECE5 D.1.3.X-CTP2)

Evidence suggests that unconventional approaches are often used in order to create the best possible conditions for the development of new knowledge which can be used for innovations. Examples of such unconventional approaches are extensive collaboration with competitors, open pricing discussions and shared invitations to networking events with central players and potential customers. Such initiatives all serve the purpose of developing the technological knowledge further and jointly position it in the minds of potential customers. However, there may be issues with legal regulations.

Looking at the strategic considerations behind these unconventional approaches, the evidence suggests that they focus, to a large extent, on how to develop the best circumstances for the exploration and exploitation of knowledge rather than specifically on how to gain the best competitive advantage. Moreover, in this sense, it is considered more valuable for the KIE ventures to collaborate extensively with all actors on the early-stage market, and jointly develop and expand the market.

Turning to the coordination of value chain activities, the location of the production competences of the KIE ventures is often in-house, as the number of products manufactured at the earlier stages of the venture creation is low and in most cases requires rigorous quality control. This suggests that the internationalization and international collaboration of KIE ventures is not driven by the benefits of outsourcing and offshoring to low-cost manufacturing countries.

The primary driver for internationalization in KIE ventures is first of all the access to new knowledge, either complementary technological knowledge or market knowledge. The KIE ventures view themselves as part of an extended knowledge network, where the synergies create advantages for all players, in step with the joint development and expansion of the markets they operate in.

Therefore, in addition to technological, scientific and market knowledge, access to social capital is also an important factor in the KIE strategy to internationalization. Social capital is seen as a ticket to be part of future interesting activities, developments and deals.

> We nurture close relationships with NASA [National Aeronautics and Space Administration], due to their influential position in relation to the funding decisions made by the Space Grant Consortium and the National Science Foundation. (Space Inc.)

Financial capital is of course also a concern for KIE ventures as they possess only scarce resources, and are often forced to prioritize their activities when engaging in internationalization. But, financial resources are not only sought through sales. They have other channels for funding, and may be able to access them in other countries, such as academic funding programmes, CVC and other capital investors. Internationalization can be seen as a necessary step in order to qualify for certain investors, and moreover, internationalization can expand access to potential funding programmes.

Access to human capital is also a prevalent consideration in relation to internationalization of KIE ventures. It is necessary to be attractive and visible in the markets where the most highly skilled people are located in order to be at the forefront of knowledge developments.

> We find the competences we need, wherever we can. Often this means looking abroad, as our technology is very advanced and specialists in our field are not easy to come by. As a matter of fact, we initiated our activities on the German market mainly due to the fact that a number of people with specialized knowledge on infra-red sensor technology are located in Germany. (Sensor Inc)

As previously discussed in this chapter, access to suitable human resources is a serious challenge for a recently started venture, and they need to be creative in their pursuit of such people.

4.5.3 Summary about Internationalization

The internationalization of KIE has illustrated a number of points. KIE face some disadvantages due to the liabilities of newness and small size, but their business development often unfolds most successfully in an international context. KIE ventures may be born global in the sense of reaching international markets and also knowledge, as illustrated in the model above. The main learning points in this section are:

- The knowledge developed through KIE often has broad international potential and, as such, efficient exploitation is best achieved on an international scale.
- Sales and low-cost manufacturing are seldom the primary reasons for KIE internationalization. Rather, during the early stages of KIE growth the knowledge generated is often dependent on input from international partners to reach a necessary maturity level to be exploited efficiently in the market.
- Once the product, technology or service reaches the appropriate maturity level to engage in sales activities, it is typical for KIE ventures to follow niche strategies, which allow them to compete in a variety of markets at an international scale.
- International activity and proven potential to reach international markets is often a requirement for investors to be seriously interested in KIE ventures.

4.5.4   Questions for Discussion

1. What are the benefits of internationalization, both in terms of benefits for the KIE venture and societal benefits?
2. What are key characteristics of KIE in an international context?
3. What are foreseeable challenges for KIE ventures when engaging in internationalization?
4. Discuss how public policy might best help KIE ventures that are interested in internationalization.

4.6   CONCLUDING REMARKS

Small firms are usually associated with simple processes and management systems, and differ significantly from large organizations. However, KIE ventures tend to manage complex processes, which supports Gartner (1985), who suggests that differences among entrepreneurs and among their ventures are as great as the variation between entrepreneurs and non-entrepreneurs and between new firms and established firms.

Hence, this chapter has introduced a more nuanced understanding of the dynamics of entrepreneurial ventures, based on the following proposition.

Significant differences exist between entrepreneurial management and general management. As one vital example, entrepreneurial management relies highly on the use of networks and emergence of access to resources. Therefore, management of KIE ventures requires a systemic understanding of processes and of the relationship between individual and context in order to design and carry out this type of entrepreneurship.

Throughout this chapter we have discussed aspects related to the management of KIE and KIE ventures and documented the dynamic interlinkages between many of these variables. Managing in this context involves leading transformation processes, which the venture undergoes as it matures and finds new directions. Management choices need to involve an understanding of the overall and interrelated dynamics of KIE ventures.

There are several ways of approaching this issue, but a key aspect of understanding the dynamics of the KIE venture is that new venture creation integrates four major perspectives in entrepreneurship: characteristics of the individual(s) who start the venture; the organization that they create; the environment surrounding the new venture; and the process by which the new venture is grown. We have specifically addressed how the interplay between internal and external sources creates very particular circumstances affecting growth, both in terms of general management practices and internationalization.

5. Evaluating performance and outputs

5.1 INTRODUCTION

This chapter describes the third phase of KIE, as related to evaluating performance and outputs of KI ventures, in relation to this proposition:

Evaluating the performance and outputs of KIE and KIE ventures requires a more nuanced understanding of how KIE can drive innovation, growth and societal development. There are different measurement techniques, and a handful of indicators are often used but may be poor indications of the performance and outputs of KIE. Moreover, at the level of KIE ventures and of society, the performance measures should include a dynamic and systemic element, as they often undergo dramatic shifts over time.

This third overall phase and topic is of great interest as the fundamental interest in KIE is based on the understanding that KIE creates positive and above-average benefits for society. That is one reason why public policy often focuses upon entrepreneurship as a means to promote growth and societal well-being. Another interest in KIE relates to the market mechanisms, and the possibility to start new companies and become millionaires in the so-called Silicon Model of the modern economy.

This chapter primarily discusses evaluating outcomes, and especially indicators and measurements of KIE. We first consider the trade-offs between quantitative and qualitative measuring techniques and indicators.

As visualized in Figure 5.1 evaluating performance and outcomes primarily relates to new firm formation, growth performance, patents and knowledge creation. After discussing each variable in turn, we address the evaluation of dynamic and systemic effects in the concluding section.

5.2 MEASURING TECHNIQUES

Measuring techniques can be either quantitative or qualitative or a study can use both types of data in a mixed method. The relative occurrence of these methods as used in studies related to KIE is discussed in the

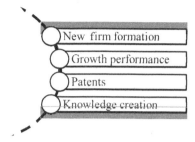

Figure 5.1   Output and performance of KIE

Appendix. Here, we wish to introduce what we are analysing, and why, as a way to illustrate concepts related to the 'believability' or validity of knowledge purporting to tell us something crucial about how and why to evaluate performance and outputs. As existing data may be insufficient, developing measuring techniques for KIE is an important task.

Taken together, the progress in the field of study of this type of entrepreneurship probably involves many researchers going back and forth between theoretical development, empirical insights through qualitative research and formal testing and modelling procedures using quantitative data.

Many research studies about entrepreneurship use a quantitative approach, primarily because it can both provide descriptive results as graphs and figures and also use statistics to test for the validity of hypotheses. We know that 20 firms were started in a high-tech sector in a specific region in Germany, or the econometrics demonstrate a correlation between starting KIE ventures and growth in that region. Qualitative studies such as case studies are also common, but they tend to illustrate a specific point to develop an understanding in order to provide empirical insight in more detail about a theoretical point. The case study may illustrate how the founder used their early networks to obtain financing resources and make links to potential customers.

For evaluating the performance and outcomes of KIE, a key issue is to think carefully about what you want to capture, and why. It seems straightforward – you want to know about the existence, growth and impact of the KIE venture. From that perspective, it should be a reasonably simple matter of determining which firms to study and how to measure their growth and knowledge creation.

However, as we have seen in earlier chapters, starting a venture is usually a long-term process. There are also multiple ownership and organizational forms. This may make a difference as to what is being examined. Some studies only examine KIE high-tech ventures that are publically traded while other studies examine all types of ownership and organizational forms. These differing choices would lead us to make different estimations of how common those types of ventures are in the economy or how many persons are employed. There are also different periods and phases involved in the evaluation. The companion case study book *How Entrepreneurs Do What They Do* provides many insights about the volatile history of individual KIE ventures, where many experience periods of rapid growth, followed by contraction (McKelvey and Lassen, 2013). Depending on which period analyzed, one may make conclusions about rapid growth in terms of employees and sales – only to find out the firm went bankrupt or was acquired by a large corporation five years later.

5.3 FOUR INDICATORS AND MEASUREMENTS OF KIE

5.3.1 New Firm Formation

New firm formation means the number of ventures started. The mere count of numbers of firms established tells us little about those firms' viability and potential for growth. Hence, the number of firms is a fairly blunt instrument, but it is widely used as a measure to indicate the existence of KIE as well as to assess and evaluate the impact of public policy.

There are questions of what types of firms are started. For reasons of comparison, data will be constructed in certain ways, and usually based upon publically available and comparative data. Many studies of the number of new firms usually focus upon the amount of new firms incorporated at all, or else, more narrowly, the quantity of new public firms on the stock market.

So when designing a study to evaluate performance – or criticizing someone else's study in terms of the validity of the results – one should first think about what exactly is being measured. What time frame? Which geographical area? Which technologies or industries? And so forth. One may also analyse the data in terms of the categories introduced in Chapter 3, namely corporate spin-off, academic spin-off and independent start-up.

5.3.2 Growth Performance

What happens next and how to measure it? In addition to starting the firm, a key indicator is related to measuring the actual performance created through growth. Growth also means broader economic growth, as discussed in Section 5.4, but here we discuss growth performance at the level of the KIE venture. Measuring the performance of new ventures is of interest because they are a major source of job creation and because improvement in performance is critical to their survival and growth.

There are a variety of measures of performance to assess growth performance and future potential. The most common include:

- annual sales
- number of employees
- return on sales
- growth in sales
- growth in employees
- financing obtained, such as venture capital.

These are the types of basic information generally available in annual reports, and some try to aggregate the data into models that take into account the likelihood of going bankrupt.

Growth performance seems straightforward but should probably be considered more explicitly as cyclical as the KIE venture evolves in the management and development phase. Many of these companies struggle to sell products and services and are instead reliant upon access to external resources. Hence, access to financing (or lack therefore) will affect the growth performance in different periods.

Of course, empirical data are not always available or consistent across industries and nations. Not all information may be available for each year of KIE venture due to differing standards of reporting and ownership structures. In addition to public registers, there are sometimes private companies that maintain databases on new firms and sell the information. Others create new data by sending questionnaires to firms or conducting a large number of interviews (usually phone-based) to collect reasonably reliable data.

In general, collecting data on the performance of new ventures is often difficult due to lack of historical information and accessibility. The same firm may also undergo periods of expansion and contraction, which leads to issues about how to measure the long-term viability of growth performance.

One way to consider the problem of data access is to evaluate different sources and methods for measuring performance. Brush and Vanderwerf (1992) found that sales figures obtained from archival sources and direct questioning of new ventures were highly and significantly correlated. Competitors proved to be a reliable third source in that the performance estimates they made were highly correlated with the estimates reported by the new ventures themselves, but their estimates sometimes differed widely in absolute value. Their study was on 66 recently formed, and high-performing manufacturing companies.

Public policy needs to keep in mind both the expected effects of growth and performance, as well as the expected timeline. This matters when an evaluation of policy occurs because many effects may take a long time, and also because the performance may vary widely in different time periods. There are also differences between models and indicators that try to explain past growth, from those that try to predict future growth – or future bankruptcy.

5.3.3   Patents and Intellectual Property Rights

Another commonly used indicator for evaluating performance and outputs is patents and IPR. Patents are often used as a proxy for measuring the output of innovation and entrepreneurship alike.

The emphasis upon this measure is based upon an idea of invention and knowledge being commodities that can be traded in a market – even if they have peculiar characteristics compared to other products and services. Patents are often used as a measure of innovation, with the assumption that the invention is both novel and relevant to business. Patents may also be used, for example, as a measure of the networks between actors, the assets of a KIE venture, the outcome of an R&D process inside a firm and so forth.

The appropriateness of this measure has continuously been a source of debate. The use of patents is often justified by the availability of cross-country and longitudinal data, which enables more rigorous comparisons over time. Patents are used in many different ways. There is literature, for example, on how patenting is an outcome from different types of KIE, such as its usefulness for firms working in areas of science and high technology. Other topics include the use of patents in relation to firm strategy for innovations, the differential reliance upon patents in different sectors and the importance of patents for future activities and performance of certain firms.

There is a finding in the AEGIS project – both in the survey and the case studies – that patents are fairly rare in European KIE ventures (Figure 5.2).

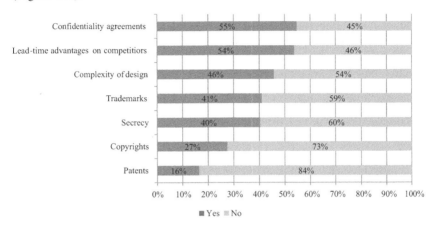

Figure 5.2   Protection of IPR in KIE ventures in Europe

This finding is also backed up by an extensive analysis of the case studies, as found in McKelvey et al. (2012). These results show that only 13 out of 86 cases studied had taken out one or more patent. Interestingly, the majority of these patenting firms are found in more traditionally low-tech industries, such as textiles and food. This is probably the reason why many of the firms operating within these low-tech industries in fact provide applications that are more of a high-tech nature. The remaining case firms applied a variety of other methods for managing their intellectual property.

Patents primarily tend to be useful for one type of firm, namely the high-tech sectors. Patents are likely to be relatively useless in capturing innovation and entrepreneurship in service sectors and to some extent in low-tech sectors. Other measures may be constructed, which could measure either the relative knowledge intensity of the firm – such as the share of skilled labour – or the relative novelty of the products – such as the percentage of sales in products introduced in the last three years. Patents may also provide a signal of quality and legitimacy for the small KIE venture.

Patents and IPR matter, and there is a huge general literature. They probably matter particularly in collaborative arrangements between partners. If the rules are not sufficiently defined between the partners, then collaborative research can end up in difficulties. Bader (2008) argued that managing intellectual property plays a crucial role in a collaborative innovation environment in that there is a need for a known and agreed upon framework. A framework matters because it provides legal protection, especially when supporting factual protection strategies that enable profits from temporary monopolies. A key question facing KIE ventures is how to manage intellectual property in the pre-phases of collaboration formation. His study focused upon information and communications technology (ICT) companies. The results are that four dominant patterns of management of IPR are identified, discussed and summarized with respect to the collaborative knowledge intensive industry environment. The four ideal types of firms and strategies are:

- The multiplicator that aims to multiply its intellectual property in R&D collaborations in order to develop knowledge for a broader market. Consequently, the multiplicator needs a strong intellectual property position that is part of a broad technology leadership.
- The leverage that aims to lever its intellectual property in R&D collaborations into narrow market sizes, such as niche markets. Similar to the multiplicator, the leverage needs a strong technology and intellectual property position.
- The absorber that aims to absorb outside intellectual property in R&D collaborations. In order to develop knowledge for a broader market, the absorber must be an attractive collaboration partner.
- The filtrator that aims to filter in missing and complementary intellectual property within R&D collaborations while approaching narrow market sizes to gain access to trusted innovators and gain collaborative, customer-specific projects.

These are interesting and different ways in which a KIE venture may use patents for managing and developing the firm rather than just as an indicator of performance.

A key debate in public policy in recent years has been focused upon patents in relation to the role of the university in society, with many attempts around the world to stimulate more patents and start-up companies from universities as a measure of the KIE activities surrounding the university.

In a meta-study, Baldini (2006) reviewed 125 papers published between 1980 and 2004 on university patenting and licensing activity in order to establish the impact of such activity on knowledge production leading to entrepreneurship. The years studied included major shifts in national institutional structures, whereby universities could take more ownership of patents and academic scientists were able to publish. Their major findings include that the surge of university patents did not happen at the expense of their quality nor of the quality of research. Moreover, scientific excellence and technology transfer activities are mutually reinforcing. Finally, they argue that university patenting and related activities need a fertile context to develop both inside and outside the campus in order to occur. This suggests, though, that academic patents are at least correlated with the starting up of university spin-offs and the broader role of the university in the knowledge economy.

Europe is doing much better than previously thought in terms of academic patents. Lissoni et al. (2008) provide summary statistics from the KEINS database on academic patenting in France, Italy and Sweden in order to assess if the acclaimed patenting gap between Europe and the US is really there. Their results show that previous assumptions that European scientists are worse than American ones at patenting are incorrect. This re-evaluation of academic patenting is offered by considering all patents signed by academic scientists active in 2004, both those assigned to universities and the many more held by business companies, governmental organizations and public laboratories. Indeed, the academic scientists in France, Italy and Sweden have invented and assigned many more patents than previously estimated, and in line with American ones in terms of percentages and technological classes. Moreover, the European academic patents tend to be assigned to firms to a high extent, suggesting that they have direct relevance for industrial invention.

The results presented in this section suggest that patents and IPR are not simply tradeable items upon a market. Instead, KIE firms can use different strategies towards IPR, even in the early phases of collaboration. Assuming that the view put forward in this book is correct – for example, that KIE ventures are highly dependent upon networks and collaboration – then thinking through and implementing a strategy in this area is essential. Patents may reflect something different than the main output of the company.

5.3.4 Knowledge Creation

Increasing attention has also been given to knowledge creation as an independent measure for output of KIE. These types of indicators are more speculative, and are related to underlying taxonomies and understandings of how KIE may work quite differently in different industries.

Knowledge creation and growth performance is likely related to the type of industry, especially if we consider the three types of high-tech industries, medium to low-tech industries and services industries. Pavitt (1984) provided a taxonomy, which suggested, inter alia, that industries share different major characteristics with regards to which actors innovate, and the type of innovations that may be useful in this context. In these three types of industries, access to knowledge sources and firm growth may be influenced by differing pressures about who is likely to be involved in innovation and the types of innovations.

In the service industries, the innovations are generally around the services provided and co-created with the customers. In contrast, science-based or high-tech industries like the pharmaceutical industry by definition do their own R&D activities, although they may also rely upon networks with others to innovate. They are focused upon product innovations.

Todtling et al. (2006) propose that knowledge intensive sectors in production and services have a lead in respect to being part of the knowledge economy, and therefore they can be considered as role models for the future. They argue that innovation process, the mechanisms of knowledge exchange and the respective linkages in those industries differ quite markedly from those in other sectors, especially in terms of clustering and local knowledge spillovers. Based on evidence from 189 Austria-based firms, their results show that knowledge-based industries seem to differ in their innovation processes from those in traditional sectors as regards key knowledge sources, the role of codified and tacit knowledge and the types of knowledge links and local clustering. For manufacturing firms, the most important knowledge sources are other firms along the value chain (customers, suppliers) including competitors. For high-tech and research firms selling services, universities are a clearly more relevant source and rely on a larger variety of knowledge inputs.

Low- and medium-tech industries tend to be more concerned with process innovations and their suppliers may do the innovating. Heidenreich (2009) finds that these firms are characterized mainly by process, organizational and marketing innovations, by weak internal innovation capabilities and a strong dependence on the external provision of machines, equipment and software. Suppliers are the most important sources for information and knowledge. Moreover, the aims of innovation activities reflect the primacy of process innovation instead of product innovation in mature industries. An increased range of goods and services and access to new markets are less important than improved flexibility of production or reduced labour costs.

The taxonomy of corporate spin-offs versus academic spin-offs is another one that may be useful for measuring knowledge creation. Let us reiterate that there is a long and ongoing debate about the relative importance of corporate spin-offs and academic spin-offs in this specific context. As such, this discussion has focused upon accessing resources and ideas through networks, but also a more recent debate that perhaps corporate spin-offs are better at creating growth but that those academic spin-offs that succeed have a more radical impact.

So another way of thinking about the impact of knowledge creation is to consider the parent organization. Let us first consider corporate spin-offs. Sapienza et al. (2004) examine the effects of knowledge relatedness on the growth after the firms have been started from industrial parent firms. The authors propose that growth is maximized when the knowledge base of the spin-off firm partially overlaps that of its parent firm. This effect is due to learning: both too small and too great an overlap will inhibit growth, the first because limited knowledge overlap hampers local search and knowledge assimilation and the second because great knowledge overlap hampers the creation of novel knowledge combinations.

Similarly, there are issues about how knowledge drives new firm formation from universities. As for universities in general, measuring the number of new firms started is a particularly poor measure for understanding the impact of universities on technological development, society and industry (Salter and Martin, 2001; Perkmann et al., 2013). Academics contribute to economic growth and social well-being through very different mechanisms, such as consultancy, diffusion of ideas and teaching. Academic engagement with industry and society is a much wider phenomenon than the simple commercialization steps of starting a company or taking a patent.

For understanding the role of universities in the knowledge economy and for individual university academics, it is not just an issue of the individual starting a company, but also a question of whether and what types of resources and support they obtain from other organizations, so there are later effects on growth performance. The university plays other roles in society than starting firms or stimulating academic entrepreneurship – and therefore it is important to understand firm formation at universities in relation to the overall missions of the modern university in a knowledge economy (Deiaco et al., 2012).

5.3.5 Reflections about Indicators and Measurements

This discussion leads us to consider new and better ways to evaluate firm formation in relation to growth performance.

Patents and IPR should be used with some care. They are useful measures for evaluating KIE in certain industries and technologies, and also for certain network measures. They are not a good proxy of innovation per se, given that translating an invention into products and services is a difficult process. Nor is it a good proxy for firms in all types of industries, and it may even be misleading to evaluate based upon this, given that many KIE ventures do not have patents. Moreover, even small KIE ventures use patents within different strategic orientations, and this will influence their propensity to patent.

Other ways would be to evaluate more complex measures such as the rate of firm formation compared to control groups, the types of firms in terms of sectors and products, the rate of survival (hazard rates) and/or average growth rates. More broadly, the economic and social impact created by new firm formation is potentially a more interesting measure, yet more rarely used due to difficulties of finding reliable statistics on impact.

There is clearly a general argument to be made about the need for a more diverse set of measures for evaluation purposes.

5.4 DYNAMIC AND SYSTEMIC EFFECTS

This section considers the evaluation of performance and outputs by considering the dynamic and systemic effects.

This last issue of dynamic and systemic effects leads us to a discussion of evaluating the actual performance and outputs at the KIE venture and societal level. These may help confirm or reject the general hypothesis that KIE drives innovation, growth and societal development. One reason this is interesting is that the measures may allow for the identification and enhancement of successful areas or industries or types of KIE as the main drivers of growth. Another is that it likewise allows for identification of areas lagging behind in this type of development, and thereby gives input to the creation of targeted initiatives to stimulate more development. These are difficult but important issues, and this section briefly introduces this overall discussion while the main focus is upon indicators and measurements.

Due to the close relationships between this type of entrepreneurship, innovation, economic growth and societal well-being, another way to expand measuring techniques is to develop new data or quantitative data to measure new phenomena. The concept of KIE is closely linked with innovativeness, as explained in Chapter 2. In the innovation literature, many indicators have been developed and could be used in the entrepreneurship literature. For example, patents are used in both, and are usually taken as a measure of invention (the act of novelty) or innovation (novelty of market value) or both. Much literature assumes that patents are a powerful and useful measurement of the commercial viability of an idea or a company. Another indicator that could be used is how well the entrepreneurial firm is doing in the market place. This is done in the innovation literature by using a taxonomy of the possible types of innovations – product, process, organizations and so forth – and asking the firm how many they have introduced in recent years. Similarly, questionnaires such as the Community Innovation Survey ask firms how much of sales is in new products innovated in the last five years as a measure of turnover of innovations inside the firm.

The reason this could be further developed is that we are particularly interested in change induced by KIE due to the overall impacts as well as the potential individual benefits. New technologies, products and services can stimulate economic growth, as well as introduce new lifestyles and change society. Product, process and organizational innovations can also help to make the production processes more efficient, potentially leading to increased capital intensity, labour productivity, and per-capita income. Often, these innovations are introduced in direct relation to KIE, either through new ventures or renewal of existing organizations.

In a broad review, Steinmueller (2011) discusses the social consequences of stimulating more entrepreneurship in society, and in doing so, reviews existing evidence about whether entrepreneurship stimulates growth, or not. He divides the results into the 'optimists' and the 'sceptics' (Steinmueller, 2011, pp, 8–9):

> There is a major division between those who argue that private sector entrepreneurship is a vital source of economic growth and development, e.g. (Braunerhjelm, Acs, Audretsch et al. 2010; Thurik 1999) and those who argue that encouraging entrepreneurship, in general, cannot be expected to bring transformation in the rate of economic growth or level of employment (Shane 2009; Storey 1982; Parker 2004).

He argues that the two sides tend to rely upon different types of economics as well as different levels of analysis. The optimists relate the formation of entrepreneurial ventures to the economic performance of regions and countries, whereas the sceptics examine the performance of the ventures. Thus, the overall economy may benefit through knowledge and spill-overs through entrepreneurial activities while it is less clear that these ventures directly create jobs and growth.

Future research could measure other types of learning outcomes rather than the simple one found here in order to further understand the dynamic and systemic effects. The indirect effect of KIE on the development of clusters and new industries seems to be a potentially interesting area. This also raises the issue of innovation in knowledge-based industries. Understanding these processes requires a detailed analysis of knowledge interactions since the firms rely to a large extent on external knowledge sources besides internal R&D.

Examples of the type of questions that need to be tackled are: Do these benefits only exist for the KIE venture created and the individual founder or for whoever becomes a millionaire? How and why does society benefit or carry the risks and costs? What types of effects should be expected and demanded by society?

6. Design thinking as a tool for entrepreneurship

6.1 DESIGNING VALUE

Design thinking has been introduced in previous chapters as a way to combine planning with uncertainty and unexpected events that occur during the process of KIE. Chapters 2, 3 and 4 have discussed various aspects of KIE and KIE ventures. They have illustrated different elements and phases of KIE, different perspectives of KIE and different ways of understanding the value created through KIE.

Throughout the discussions, a number of concepts have continuously arisen as essential to the understanding of KIE. Among these are emergence and proactivity in relation to all aspects of KIE venturing. But what exactly do emergence and proactivity teach us about how to understand KIE and engage in orchestrating knowledge in entrepreneurial ventures ourselves? In this chapter we address such questions, which are related to the sixth proposition of the book:

Our view is that design thinking can be developed and utilized to play an important role for the successful exploration and exploitation of KIE. Without this, there is a lack of tools and techniques to manage tensions between creativity and order or structure. With this, we can develop a systemic approach to shaping the thinking about venture creation and innovation for developing KIE ventures.

Generally speaking, two common perspectives prevail on how to act to create value through entrepreneurship. One perspective emphasizes novelty, intuitive thinking and creativity. The other attaches importance to analytical thinking, logic and certainty. This difference in perspectives is also visible through the fact that businesses generally emphasize either exploration (seeking, creating and generating something new) or exploitation (focusing on creating profits out of what already exists).

Both are legitimate ways to generate value, but each carries risks for the KIE venture. If you overemphasize exploration, the KIE venture will not be stable, and a sustainable cash flow will not be generated, making the venture highly vulnerable. On the other hand, emphasizing only exploitation, which at first increases efficiency and cuts costs, will eventually lead you to a point of diminishing returns on your existing products, and it will increase the risks of someone else creating a new product that will displace you. When reading literature on entrepreneurship and management, you are often led to the conclusion that successful business managers and entrepreneurs must choose between such perspectives. And indeed on the surface, the two perspectives may seem rather irreconcilable.

However, design thinking offers a third alternative, which we propose is very well suited for understanding and engaging in the processes involved in KIE venturing. The heart of the design thinking process lies at the intersection of technical feasibility, economic viability and desirability by the user, which, as illustrated throughout this book, is also where we find the interrelated and interdependent aspects of KIE. As such, what we propose is that KIE is not the result of sudden breakthroughs or strikes of genius; it is a result of hard work augmented by a creative discovery process and followed by iterative cycles of prototyping, testing and refinement.

Thus, applying design thinking to KIE could be a powerful way of framing opportunities, understanding how KIE unfolds and even gaining insight into specific tools and methods that allow experimentation. In the context of this book, design represents a way of thinking about and bringing together elements, which can jointly be part of a process in order to provide solutions for society.

6.2   WHAT IS DESIGN THINKING?

In 1969, modern day philosopher Herbert Simon in his book *Sciences of the Artificial* called for increased knowledge about design processes as a means of approaching business problems. Much of the thinking has been applied in engineering and management approaches to problem solving. With the recent introduction of effectuation theory to the study of entrepreneurship, this discussion has also taken root within entrepreneurship. Sarasvathy (2008) introduced the idea of entrepreneurship as the design of novel artefacts; the entrepreneur is faced with the challenge of envisioning the future and designing novel artefacts. Hence, the development of an opportunity is essentially 'a problem of designing without a final goal' (Sarasvathy, 2001, p. 523). She thus suggests that design thinking will aid the entrepreneur in exploring and exploiting innovative opportunities. Methods and processes of designing opportunities are explained by Sarasvathy (2008, p. 186) as follows:

> The pragmatist effectuator will look carefully at the actual world and figure out courses of action, however local and contingent, that are both doable and worth doing. Then, through interactions with others, effectuators will redefine the designs of their solutions.

As this quote indicates, the potential of design thinking for KIE has been recognized for a while.

The contribution of this chapter is to focus on how design thinking can be used to combine the scientific principles discussed for learning about this type of entrepreneurship with the hands-on experience of engaging in it. Currently, only limited explanations exist about the actual methods of designing entrepreneurship, and the challenge for companies is to not only think in a design manner, but also act in such a manner (Nielsen et al., 2012).

Hence, this chapter collects a number of insights from design literature about how designers go about exploring and exploiting new opportunities. The following outlines different perspectives on design practices and gives specific examples of design methods and tools. These methods and tools will by no means offer a complete picture of design tools, but are chosen to give the reader inspiration to try out specific design methods and tools that can aid the doing of KIE.

6.2.1   Different Approaches to Design Thinking

Historically, design has been treated as a downstream activity in the development process; the point where designers, who have played no earlier role in the innovation process, are involved to create an aesthetic frame for the idea. However, in particular since the 1980s, the concept of design has become an increasingly valuable competitive asset in, for example, the consumer electronics, automotive and consumer packaged goods industries. In parallel to this, design thinking has also experienced a reflective turn; design is now considered a reflective practice within a more comprehensive, process-oriented and interactive space (Bousbaci, 2008).

With these developments, it is possible to identify several generations of perspectives on design thinking. First-generation design thinking reflects a rational and logical design process, whereas the second and third generations emphasize design as a problem-solving process of bounded rationality. The generations differ in terms of how they view the nature of the 'opportunity' in question. In first-generation design thinking it is a straightforward matter of solving a specific problem by creating the right solution. In later generation design thinking, it is an emergent process where the opportunities arise through the continuous interaction between problems and solutions.

This difference in perspective on the nature of opportunities is also found in entrepreneurship literature as developed in this book. In short, the discussions here about opportunities are generally divided into two perspectives: a perception of opportunities as Kirznerian activities of discovery and alertness as opposed to a Schumpeterian view of opportunities as involving creation (Shane, 2003). The major difference between the discovery-oriented perspective (Kirznerian) and creation-oriented perspective (Schumpeterian) is whether opportunities exist a priori, waiting for the alert entrepreneur to recognize and exploit them, or if opportunities are created and willed into existence by the entrepreneur through exploration. Opportunities, in the Schumpeterian view, emerge out of the entrepreneur's internal disposition to initiate changes in the economy, as well as in his or her ability to create new combinations. This is referred to as a process of creative destruction where the entrepreneur does not discover opportunities, but rather, creates them through technological change and innovation, and thus from novel knowledge and information (Schumpeter, 1934).

First-generation design thinking and processes typically follow a Kirznerian view on opportunities. The design process is said to 'begin with the acknowledgement of needs, dissatisfaction with current state of affairs, and realization that some action must take place in order to correct the problem' (Braha and Maimon, 1997, p. 147). The concrete problem (market gap, user need and so on) that the designer wants to solve is in this way clearly defined at the beginning of the design process. This perspective on the design process reflects an efficiency focus on design, often with a strong user and market orientation. In this sense, the opportunity determines the design process, as the designer engages in a systematic and structured search for solutions to the problem.

Second- and third-generation design thinking depart from the notion that in most design processes it is not possible to identify the problem or opportunity up-front (Sebastian, 2005). The problem is simply too complex, ill-defined and vague to be completely understood from the beginning of the design process. As such, the designer must act much more in line with a Schumpeterian view on opportunities. This is where we start seeing a clear parallel to KIE as presented in this book, and especially when we consider how knowledge intensive entrepreneurs go about creating ventures. The understanding of the problem arises through emergent activities of designing solutions, concepts, prototypes and so on. And even then the problem will constantly change. Rittel (1972) and later Buchanan (1992) describe this as design processes aimed at solving an unframed or 'wicked' problem, referring back to a previous definition as

> problems which are ill-formulated, where the information is confusing, where there are many clients and decision makers with conflicting values and where the ramifications in the whole system are thoroughly confusing. (Rittel quoted in Buchanan, 1995)

According to De Bono (1978, p. 139) dealing with wicked problems involves moving 'from idea to idea until something begins to look promising'. Thus, the design process becomes the deliberate process of designing innovative opportunities based on linking emerging actions, resources, people, requirements, knowledge and so on (Dorst, 2006). This is a process in which new ideas emerge, are combined and change over time, and this book has demonstrated how and why these processes involve the mobilization of resources from a wide variety of actors from inside and outside the organization.

Similar ideas are discussed by, for example, Clausen and Yoshinaka (2007) who describe the design process as a space within the boundaries of a particular topic, and a way to explore the problems and solutions of the space is to invite many different participants with different points of view, knowledge and practices into the space. Lawson (1980) further argued that the nature of design is that problems cannot be comprehensively stated, and that any statement of a problem requires subjective interpretation on the part of the designer. Solutions are innumerable and there is never one that is optimal. The design process is endless, with no infallibly correct methodology. Therefore, design begins by being a conjecture, and after utilization, a modification job that involves finding as well as solving problems.

In practice, this change in perception of design thinking to the third-generation perspective has consequences for the role of the designer. Now, rather than asking designers to make an already developed idea more attractive to consumers, companies are asking them to create ideas that better meet consumers' needs and desires. For example, one of the best known design houses IDEO in Palo Alto (http://www.ideo.com) now explicitly phrases their role as designers under the headings: 'We help organizations innovate; We help organizations grow; We help organizations build businesses; We help organizations develop capabilities'. These statements show that IDEO clearly consider it as part of their design competences to be innovative and entrepreneurial. This illustrates the argument presented in this book that design thinking and design competences are useful to stimulate KIE.

6.2.2 Design Thinking and KIE

Given the multiple specific approaches to design, this literature provides insights, which this book has used to understand KIE as a design process generating something better or different compared to what already exists. It is as an action aimed at transforming the present into a preferred and more desirable future situation (Orlikowski, 2004).

For example, Lindberg et al. (2011) describe the steps taking place during a design process in terms of tackling a given problem by exploring its problem space with hands-on research (for example, by inquiries, interviews, observations, self-experiments), exploring its solution space with various ideating techniques (for example, by brainstorming, sketching, prototyping) and aligning the ideas with reality through repeated feedback that helps to refine or revise the selected paths towards a solution. In Figure 6.1 we illustrate this process, which also helps us understand the dynamics of the KIE model presented in this book.

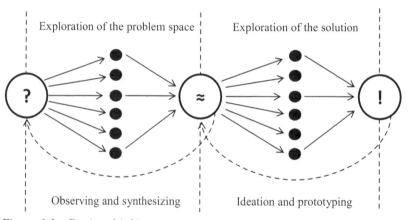

Figure 6.1   Design thinking

When exploring a problem space, design thinking involves an intuitive (and not fully verbalized) understanding, mainly by observing cases or scenarios, as opposed to formulating general hypotheses or theories regarding the problem, and synthesizing such knowledge into specific points of view. The specific points of view serve as entry points into creating a great number of alternative ideas in parallel and into elaborating them with sketching and prototyping techniques. In this manner, ideas are being consciously transformed into tangible ideas and ways forward.

In the KIE creation model (see Figure 2.3) we also see how the variables at the different stages are interrelated, and move forward based on iteration. The specific steps suggested by design thinking provide more practical input to how such iterations take place in practice. Many knowledge intensive entrepreneurs perform these steps rather intuitively, but could potentially benefit from making their design approach an an explicit part of the KIE process, which was one rationale for writing this book. The more tangible the ideas are, the easier they are to communicate. And as we have seen in all phases of the KIE creation model, communication and interaction with external sources is often essential to acquire resources, to gain new knowledge, to gain validity and to gain market access. These representations of ideas and concepts facilitate communication not only in the KIE venture, but also with venture capitalists, users, clients and other experts.

Design thinking thus gives us a foundation for thinking about KIE as a process of designing innovative opportunities, through the interactions between the founder, the KIE venture, and the external environment as proposed in this book. Design thinking can be used to specify more explicit steps of development, and the reader can use that understanding to see how the founder and firm should engage in dynamic interplay between the different phases and second-order variables defined in the KIE creation model. Moreover, it can help us understand that while combining different types of knowledge is necessary, but difficult to do, finding explicit design processes for interactions amongst stakeholders may lead to a better translation of knowledge into opportunities for the firm. Finally, some of the tools and techniques may help provide explicit management techniques that can be used to actively design innovative opportunities, by combining different types of knowledge in the exploration and exploitation phases.

In particular, the process of constant iterations between addressing problems and creating solutions is very visible in the evidence on KIE presented throughout this book. The process is at best described metaphorically as a system of spaces rather than a predefined series of orderly steps. The spaces demarcate different sorts of related activities that together form the continuum of exploration and exploitation of an innovative opportunity. This approach is clearly one of the aspects that differentiate the KIE described here from other approaches to entrepreneurship. For example, in Chapter 3, we can see this in relation to the particular traits and cognition of the knowledge intensive entrepreneur, especially how financing is obtained from a variety of sources and through different means; in Chapter 4 on the creative approaches to knowledge acquisition and utilization in KIEs; and in Chapter 5 on how KIE eventually creates value at several different levels, beyond the mere establishment of new ventures. These variables are all heavily influenced by the abilities of the knowledge intensive entrepreneurs to continuously explore both problem spaces and solution spaces. This way of thinking about problems and solutions also helps explain why emergence and proactivity are two of the essential aspects of KIE as proposed in this book.

6.3   TOOLS AND TECHNIQUES FOR DESIGN THINKING

In addition to providing a way of thinking about KIE, design thinking also points to a number of tools and techniques useful for enhancing the practical insights into KIE. These may be useful in all three phases of the KIE creation model. Such tools and techniques are developed based on a range of methods from what is referred to as the creative design literature (for example, Crilly, 2010). This literature pays special attention to creativity as an essential element of any design process (Cross, 1997; Dorst and Cross, 2001), which is possible to stimulate through the deliberate application of creative methods and processes (Ryhammar and Brolin, 1999). It reveals a wealth of different methods and processes relevant for designing KIE as it deals with 'how designers work, how they think, and how they carry out design activity' (Bayazit, 2004, p. 16).

This section introduces a number of such methods in order for the reader to contemplate how to go about utilizing the scientific knowledge of KIE as a general phenomena in a practical setting, as discussed in this book. However, bear in mind that the introduction of such methods is not to suggest that knowledge intensive entrepreneurs actually make explicit use of these tools in their approach to KIE. Rather, the purpose is to give the reader a number of suggestions on how to experiment with the understanding of design and redesign of interrelated systems, in order to help entrepreneurs better manage their business. Hence, not all tools are directly applicable when considering KIE and venture creation, but all are based on principles that teach us about the design thinking mindset needed in order to be able to understand and conduct KIE in practice.

As such, the tools all have central elements in common, which aid us in moving from a conceptual understanding of KIE towards a more practical understanding. All of the methods build on the logic of iterative exploration of problem and solutions spaces presented in Figure 6.1. The elements of specific relevance to the KIE creation model are further elaborated in Figure 6.2.

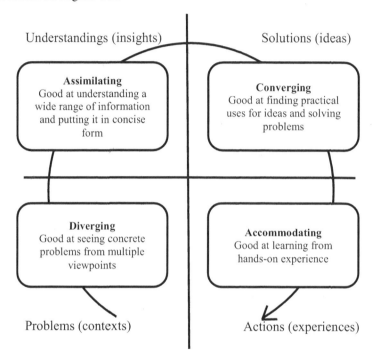

Understandings (insights)　　　　Solutions (ideas)

Assimilating
Good at understanding a wide range of information and putting it in concise form

Converging
Good at finding practical uses for ideas and solving problems

Diverging
Good at seeing concrete problems from multiple viewpoints

Accommodating
Good at learning from hands-on experience

Problems (contexts)　　　　Actions (experiences)

Figure 6.2　Designing KIE

This model shows the interrelatedness of divergent and convergent thinking, which is mediated and driven forward by action, tangible artefacts and understanding, as well as the iterative nature of such elements.

It is also worth noting that many experienced designers actually find themselves following such processes so intuitively that they hardly recognize it as a systematic approach. For example, Swann (2002) describes how a founding partner of Pentagram (one of the world's largest independent design consultancies) clearly operates within the process outlined in Figure 6.2, but is acutely aware that this is a highly intuitive process:

> For myself, I try to sum up the situation, back in edgeways, and cast around for ideas on which to hang further ideas. It's an intuitive process involving search, discovery, recognition, and evaluation. Rejection or development. There are no specific rules or recipes. One might slip through a sequence of actions in seconds, sweat through step by step, start backwards, move randomly from one point to another, or do what surfers call 'hang ten' – get your toes in the board and ride the crest of the wave.

The tools we introduce are all used in practice by designers and are easily related to the models presented in Figures 6.1 and 6.2. When discussing each tool, we also point out the relationship to the KIE creation model.

6.3.1 Participatory Design

Participatory design principles are used in the development of products, technologies and services. The aim of participatory design is to develop more responsive approaches to user needs. Over the last decade, the user-centric aspect of participatory design has increased immensely. The rise of participatory design moves the focus from the traditional concept of design as an individual creative activity towards design as being a collaborative creative activity in which users participate. This kind of participation is aimed at achieving design results that match the needs of the prospective users.

In such a process, the users are not just involved as a source of information, or an input for the work of the designers, but participate as designers themselves. There are great benefits in adopting this approach; not only does it achieve a match between the design and the user needs, but it also achieves user buy-in for the design solution. Because it is also created from the very early stages of the design process, this has significant positive effects on the eventual market implementation. An example of how participatory design is applied in practice is seen in the Danish project InnoDoors, which actively integrates users into the innovation processes in the construction material industry (see http://www.innodoors.dk for more information). The local Danish users and producers interact in person and electronically, in order to develop construction materials that are appropriate for the local context. This project shows that participatory design methods are highly empowering for the participants, since they have a creative opportunity to express their opinion as part of a design project that is interested in what they have to say.

In relation to the KIE creation model, participatory design principles can help the venture to develop relevant products and services. This method can be a way to define how the technological, scientific and creative knowledge held by the KIE venture may be translated into products and services desired by the users. This tool may be useful early on – when accessing resources and ideas as inputs – as well as in the later phase of managing and developing the KIE venture.

6.3.2 LEGO Serious Play™

LEGO Serious Play™ (LSP) was developed in the mid-1990s as a specific in-company executive education programme in the LEGO Company (Roos et al., 2004). LSP was developed based on the realization that people through active small-scale physical experiments were able to express their thoughts and creativity in a highly constructive manner. Moreover, by doing so in collaboration, the participants not only created innovative ideas, but also engaged in a joint understanding of the problem and solution spaces, which eased further development processes.

LSP as a design and learning method uses LEGO™ bricks to enable the players to take a speedy shortcut to the core of the problem and build a solution in collaboration with other co-players. The bricks work as a catalyst for creating a tangible image of participants' thoughts, and when used for building metaphors, they can trigger processes that are otherwise either difficult or make explicit. LEGO bricks are in this way used for facilitating thinking, communication and problem solving within organizations, teams and individuals. The basic assumption of LSP is that the answers to whichever issue is at stake are already present among the participants, and just need to be made tangible. The method invites participants to 'think with their hands' as opposed to idea generation being a strictly mental process. The core process of at least a one-day LSP learning workshop is based on four essential steps:

1. Posing the question. The participants are challenged by a question that should have no obvious or correct solution. This stimulates the participants to start thinking divergently about the problem.
2. Construct. The participants make sense of what they know and what they can imagine by constructing a model using LEGO bricks and materials. They develop a story of the way they understand the problem, and the solution spaces they imagine. Through this process they construct new knowledge in their mind.

3.   Sharing. The stories are shared between the participants. The process of building something physical with the hands, which is then discussed, can lead to much more insightful discussions. New perspectives can be unlocked if people build something in a creative, reflective process. The building of items is only one side of the process. The items are only metaphors for meaning. The meaning can easily be grasped by the other team members, and feedback questions can be asked.

4.   Reflecting. As a way of internalizing and grounding the story, reflection upon what was heard or seen in the model is encouraged. After the process of expressing the individual meanings, the models can also be put together into a shared model – representing the collectively shared object of work or research. Such an object may represent the actual status of work reality. It can, however, be developed towards future visions.

This method has been applied with great success in a variety of studies in many different areas such as business, sociology and psychology. Until 2010, the LEGO Corporation offered the tool through a network of licensed facilitators trained in using the method. However, since then LEGO has launched an open source model, in recognition of the very diverse areas of application and varieties in interest. For further inspiration we refer the reader to www.seriousplay.com.

Among the frequent users of LSP is, for example, Swiss-based Imagination Lab (http://www.imagilab.org). They utilize LSP in their work on how to foster imagination in business decisions and strategy. Said and Roos (2002) argue that one of the powerful aspects of LSP is that it offers the possibility to create a common language between all participants, thereby easing the communication of novel ideas. LSP is also often applied in research published in academic journals focusing on the benefits of visual and tangible methods; for example, Visual Studies by the International Visual Sociology Association.

LSP could be used internally within the KIE venture, particularly in relation to managing and developing the company. As discussed in Chapter 4, this phase often requires significant trade-offs and challenges related to how to organize and focus the venture towards goals. LSP could provide shared views of the future and ways to solve the conflicts and trade-offs involved in prioritizing different kinds of knowledge and between exploration and exploitation.

6.3.3 Ethnographic Film and Photography

Visualization can also be a tool. As noted by Grady (1996), there is a strong reflexive relationship between ideas and visible materials, and visible things become important to understand culture and social life. Because pictures help us capture details otherwise overlooked, they help us look at opportunities with different eyes. Photography and videotaping are tools that have been much used for a long time by ethnographers and sociologists. As design has changed towards increasingly understanding user needs and future trends, so has the use of such tools expanded.

In KIE, the use of visualization techniques is useful at several different stages. It is useful in connection with the initial ideation processes as a way to better capture, understand and discuss different needs and opportunities. It could also be a strong tool to use as part of the communication process involved in attracting initial resources to the KIE venture (as discussed in Chapter 3); guiding the development process of the KIE venture (as discussed in Chapter 4); or demonstrating and communicating the results created in the KIE venture (as discussed in Chapter 5).

A good place to look for further inspiration on the use of visualization in different ways and for different purposes is in van Leeuwen and Jewitt's *Handbook of Visual Analysis* (2000), which is a multidisciplinary edited collection with examples of visual research methods from psychology, semiotics, cultural studies, anthropology and media studies.

6.3.4 Rapid Prototyping

Prototyping is generally thought of as being complex and expensive, but it does not have to be so. New techniques focus upon rapid cycles of prototyping and more recently through 3D printing. Brown (2008) provides a good example of this in his description of one of IDEO's design projects. He describes how IDEO helps a group of surgeons develop a new device for sinus surgery. While the surgeons describe the ideal physical characteristics of the device, one of the designers uses a whiteboard marker, a film canister and a clothespin and tapes them together to illustrate the device described. With this rough prototype in hand, the surgeons are hereafter able to be much more precise about what the ultimate design should accomplish.

This example illustrates that prototyping should take only as much time, effort and investment as needed in order to receive useful feedback and evolve an idea. The more complete a prototype seems, the less likely it is that the developers will pay attention to and profit from feedback. Hence, the goal of prototyping is not to finish the product. It is to learn about the strengths and weaknesses of the idea and identify new directions that further prototypes might take. In relation to KIE ventures, this could be a way to help users become involved in designing products and services, and particularly in cases where it is ambiguous about how to apply the technological, scientific and creative knowledge within the venture.

6.3.5   Tangible Business Process Modelling

Product design thinking has also been applied to business processes. As described above, the use of low-cost physical prototypes is considered a very successful method in innovative practices for product design. In particular, early and repetitive involvement of users is responsible for the success of these methods.

Tangible Business Process Modelling (TBPM) is a mixed-methods approach to create and test different business processes in a high frequency of iterations. As such, this tool may be applied in established organizations (with existing business processes) or in KIE ventures (where business processes are to be designed and established).

The basis of TBPM is to create a way to make business process models that are tangible, and this is based on similar principles as regular board games. In general, the elements of the game consist of basic shapes of all elements for control and data flow. Flow itself and resource allocation (pools and lanes) are drawn directly on the table. The rules associated with the different shapes focus the discussion and push the participants to frame their output into the concepts of control flow, data flow and resources. They can easily create, delete, arrange and rearrange objects. This modelling tool bears many of the same characteristics as LEGO Serious Play, especially the strong emphasis on making the intangible tangible, involving multiple actors, facilitating easy change and creating an overview of interrelated elements. These are all characteristics that we can easily associate with KIE and why the tool is considered a good way of experimenting with the phase of managing and developing the KIE venture.

6.3.6   SCRUM

SCRUM is a technique first developed in the area of software engineering with many varieties of SCRUM available via the internet and via certification, as well as many different types of electronic project management tools. However, the usability of such tools in other fields is high, as they reflect an approach where the development process is complicated and complex, and where maximum flexibility and appropriate control is required. SCRUM is specifically developed to enable software development teams to operate adaptively within a complex environment using imprecise processes. The closer the development team operates to the edge of chaos, while still maintaining order, the more competitive and useful the resulting system will be. SCRUM is developed on the principles that fast iterations, constant communication and forward movement are key. In fact, forward movement is often prioritized higher than complete answers and results in recognition of the fact that the answers and results will most likely change as the development progresses. SCRUM consists of the following phases:

Pre-game: Planning. If a new idea is being developed, this phase consists of both conceptualization and analysis. If an existing idea is being enhanced, this phase consists of limited analysis. The definition of a new release includes only an estimate of its schedule and cost.

Architecture: Design. How the items of the backlog (that is, prioritized features list) will be implemented. This phase includes, for example, product architecture modification and high-level design.

Game: Development sprints. The actual development happens in 'sprints' with constant respect to the variables of time, requirements, quality, cost and competition. There are multiple, iterative development sprints, or cycles, that are used to evolve the system.

Post-game: Closure. This phase includes preparation for product release, final documentation, staged testing and actual release.

SCRUM has the distinct advantage that prototypes are developed rapidly and continuously. The tool moves attention away from the idea of creating complete or perfect solutions, and towards the idea of creating usable solutions through which learning is achieved.

The most important features are:

- Small teams – each team has no more than six members. There may be multiple teams within a project.
- Frequent reviews – team progress is reviewed as frequently as environmental complexity and risk dictates (usually one to four weeks).
- Collaboration – intra- and inter-collaboration is expected during the project.
- Object oriented.

The high focus on iterations in SCRUM is also reflected in the approach of the knowledge intensive entrepreneur in establishing and growing the venture. As distinct from managers whose work flow is centred on ongoing, permanent assignments, knowledge intensive entrepreneurs work on a 'project' basis. By this we mean that the young age of the KIE venture and the constant presence of possible failure cause the entrepreneur to continuously work on short-term activities (for example, the next sale, the next feature of the product or the next person to hire) to ensure long-term growth.

As a result, knowledge intensive entrepreneurs are accustomed to forming ad hoc teams and collaborating for specific purposes and can apply the SCRUM principles. The founders view the KIE development as an accumulation of the 'projects' they work on rather than the consequence of following a strategic plan. Whereas managers in mature organizations avoid working with wicked problems, knowledge intensive entrepreneurs embrace these problems as a challenge. In conventional management thinking, constraints are seen as an undesirable barrier to the generation and implementation of ideas; for the knowledge intensive entrepreneur, however, constraints are embraced as an impetus to creative solutions. This approach to development allows knowledge intensive entrepreneurs to deal with wicked problems as they move from idea to idea until something begins to look promising (De Bono, 1978).

6.3.7   Scenario Planning

Scenario planning is the last technique included in this chapter. Scenario planning is a structured way to think about a variety of different possible futures, and thereby the future can be explored as the development of the project or organization on navigation between these scenarios. This technique can also be used to integrate several of the other tools discussed, for example, LSP or rapid prototyping could be tools supporting the development of different scenarios. In Peter Schwartz's book *The Art of the Long View* (1991, p. 3), scenarios are described as:

> Stories that can help us recognize and adapt to changing aspects of our present environment. They form a method for articulating the different pathways that might exist for you tomorrow, and finding your appropriate movements down each of those possible paths.

Scenario planning as a technique did not emerge from design, but primarily from disciplines focused on decision-making. However, design practice has been very successful in adopting this technique into the range of approaches applied by designers. Scenario planning has been used by some of the world's largest corporations, including Royal Dutch Shell, Motorola, Disney and Accenture (Huss and Honton, 1987). In addition to these large corporations, the scenario planning technique is also very suitable for KIE ventures. The reason is that scenario planning helps in confronting uncertainty about how the future might unfold and how this might affect the organization, and KIE ventures in particular operate under such uncertainties.

Numerous variations of scenario planning exist, each identifying a number of discrete steps, varying from five to 15 or more, depending on what features of scenarios are highlighted or ignored. Some consultancies have even elaborated and branded specific scenario models, for example, Future Mapping by Northeast Consulting Resources Inc. and TAIDA (an acronym for 'Tracking, Analysing, Imaging, Deciding, Acting'), developed at Kairos Future in Sweden.

The steps suggested in such scenario models are in fact rather simple. For example, Huss and Honton (1987) describe one approach as being:

- analysing the concerns/problem space
- identifying the key decision factors
- identifying the key environmental forces
- analysing the environmental forces
- defining scenario logics
- elaborating the scenarios
- analysing implications for key decision factors
- analysing implications for decisions and strategies.

For all scenario planning techniques the process essentially involves asking and trying to answer a number of questions, such as:

1.   What can and might happen in the market?
2.   What can I do?
3.   What am I going to do?
4.   How am I going to do it?

For many entrepreneurs these questions will most likely also be influenced by questions such as: Who am I? What are my values? What do I really feel like doing?

As discussed in Chapter 3, KIE is often highly influenced by the personal preferences, knowledge and motivation of the individual entrepreneurs. This is also nicely illustrated in several of the case studies in the companion book *How Entrepreneurs Do What They Do: Case Studies of Knowledge Intensive Entrepreneurship* (McKelvey and Lassen, 2013*)*. For example, in Chapter 8 of that book, a case is presented on how two entrepreneurs, co-founders of a digital advertising agency in a small European country, during two turbulent decades seize numerous opportunities through their actions, interactions and personal drive.

One of the key strengths that scenario planning could have for KIE is the structured approach to discussing, visualizing and communicating uncertainties. This is an inherent part of KIE, which often leads to failure if not addressed properly. Scenario planning offers such an intentional approach to doing so.

6.4   CONCLUDING REMARKS

Throughout this chapter we have discussed how design thinking helps us better understand the practical creation and development of knowledge intensive ventures. This is a theme seldom addressed directly in academic books, but one that we consider essential in order to truly bridge the gap between academic knowledge and practical application of knowledge. As such, the aim of this chapter has been to relate the proposed conceptual KIE creation model to actual ways of implementing KIE in practice through design thinking methods and techniques. This provides the final link between evidence of KIE, conceptual and theoretical frameworks about KIE and application of theory through implementation of KIE.

7. Societal impacts of knowledge intensive entrepreneurship and the role of public policy

7.1 INTRODUCTION

This chapter concludes this book with insights and critical reflections about the societal impacts of KIE and the role of public policy. This chapter thus addresses the last proposition introduced in Chapter 1 about the broader role of KIE in economic growth and social well-being, and how public policy can influence these processes:

A key issue is how and why to develop public policy and societal influences that are important for being able to explain, and stimulate, KIE processes and phenomena. The broader societal context explicitly affecting the development and formation of KIE ventures especially includes knowledge, markets, institutions and opportunities. Just as design thinking provides tools at the level of the KIE venture, public policy also has tools and recommendations about how to encourage and support this type of entrepreneurship.

This broader perspective starts from our understanding of how KIE ventures interact with the external environment and ecosystem. Entrepreneurship is more than knowing how to build a company because it represents a line of thinking about how to shape business and society. Entrepreneurship is affected by the external environment, which consists of knowledge, markets, institutions and opportunities. The external environment provides inputs for resources and ideas that can be accessed by the firm, but strategy and decision-making inside the venture also matter. Thus, this book has shown how and why specific choices in the internal development and management phases of the KIE venture lead them to interpret and combine these resources and ideas into products and services.

For politicians and others engaged in public policy, a key issue is how to understand and introduce policy tools and instruments in order to stimulate and direct KIE in ways beneficial for society as a whole. Thus, talking about societal impacts and the role of public policy means that we need to understand the links between what happens within specific KIE ventures and the broader external environment and ecosystem. Society and public policy need to capture the positive dynamic effects and value created for society through entrepreneurship, and try to avoid negative outcomes. The key issues are what types of venture creation should be stimulated, how knowledge is translated into value and what types of policy goals and instruments are effective. These are very big and challenging issues that should be tackled through dialogue, which can combine more detailed research with deep insights generated by policy-makers active in these fields. This chapter will only focus upon discussing societal impacts, and the implications of our conceptual view of KIE, as related to how and why societal impacts may act to encourage and support this type of entrepreneurship.

The chapter first discusses how the links work in practice, between what happens within specific KIE ventures and the broader external environment and ecosystem. Examples are used from the companion book *How Entrepreneurs Do What They Do: Case Studies in Knowledge Intensive Entrepreneurship* (McKelvey and Lassen, 2013). These 13 case studies illustrate in detail what happens along the way.

Subsequent sections address societal impacts and implications for thinking about public policy, following the three phases of the KIE creation model. Section 7.2 examines the practice of KIE, when we follow how entrepreneurs start their firms and access knowledge and resources. Section 7.3 discusses the early stage of accessing resources and ideas, while Section 7.4 turns to the development and management phase and Section 7.5 to the evaluation of performance.

7.2   IN PRACTICE

This section returns to the practice of KIE, by first providing an overview of KIE case studies covered in *How Entrepreneurs Do What They Do* and then discussing them in light of three issues that were introduced in Chapter 1 of this book. These three issues are relevant to consider before making public policy recommendations and designing policy instruments related to the specific phases. The underlying understanding of the phenomena and processes found in the KIE creation model can moderate how quickly, or directly, public policy can affect societal impacts. The first issue is the balancing and trade-offs between business planning and uncertainty. The second issue is which types of KIE ventures to stimulate. And the third issue is how KIE ventures interact with the external environment to create and realize innovative opportunities. This includes accessing resources and ideas relevant to the three types of knowledge: scientific, technological and creative; market; and business.

An overview of the case studies in *How Entrepreneurs Do What They Do* is initially provided. They are grouped into the broad sectoral categories, 'Transversal Technologies, Engineering and Software', 'Lifestyle Technologies' and 'Human Health Care and Food'. Each case study provides interesting empirical material and has been characterized by a series of variables, useful for understanding the KIE phenomena and processes. The three broad sectors can be defined as follows:

'Transversal Technologies, Engineering and Software' refers to technologies that are useful across a range of applications or uses, and they also represent sectors in the economy. These technologies are often adaptable to different products and services. The case studies address the aspects shown in Table 7.1.

'Lifestyle Technologies' represents firms and industries involved in technologies that are used in and help develop modern society. In the digital society, many people invest in lifestyle and experiences, which are generally facilitated by IT and telecommunications. Such contemporary technologies offer more flexible forms of social and economic activity, whereby the advanced nations begin exhibiting lifestyle-led and leisure-oriented development of society. An overview of the case studies is shown in Table 7.2.

'Human Health Care and Food' represents sectors that seem both extremely localized regionally and nationally in terms of delivery of services, but also global in terms of ownerships and markets. They may also be very high-tech and quite low-tech simultaneously, depending upon where one looks in the global supply chains and innovation processes. These sectors will need much innovation in the future, in order to solve grand societal challenges like ageing populations and environmental degradation. These case studies are outlined in Table 7.3.

Table 7.1   Case studies in 'Transversal Technologies, Engineering and Software'

Case no.	1	2	3	4	5
KIE phase	Founding; development; effects and performance	Development	Founding; development	Development	Development
Focus	Development of network relationships	Interaction of KIE with university centres	Financing and development of KIE	Opportunity development; application of knowledge resources globally	Development of network relationships
Industry	Sensor technology	Engineering	Software	Wind turbines	Nano satellite technology
Founding date	2009	10-year period	1999	2009–11 (period in focus)	2007
Number of employees	12	Academic spin-offs	NA	Europe 140 in 2011, China 12 in 2011	7
Geographical area	Europe	Europe	Europe	Europe/China	Worldwide
Main product	Gas sensors	NA	Industrial software	Ready to install composite material-based solutions for wind turbine and construction industries	Nano satellite
Network involves universities?	Yes	Yes	NA	No	Yes
Network involves customers?	Yes	Yes	Yes	Yes	Yes
Network involves public policy /actors?	Yes	Yes	NA	No	Yes

Table 7.2   Case studies in 'Lifestyle Technologies'

Case no.	6	7	8
KIE phase	Founding	Founding; development, effects	Founding; development (to some extent)
Focus	Spin-off activities based on the knowledge base in a high-tech cluster	Creative destruction and ambiguity of knowledge	Identifying the various modes of entry and discussing the challenges for KIE to enter in particular industries
Industry	Wireless communication cluster	Digital advertising	European steel roller coaster industry
Founding date	2000	1994–2010	1953–2011
Number of employees	4500	34 (2009)	38 firms (number of employees vary from 20 to 300+)
Geographical area	Europe	Europe	Europe
Main product	Wireless communication-related products and services	Digital advertising campaigns	Steel roller coasters
Network involves universities?	Yes	No	No
Network involves customers?	Yes	Yes	Yes, indirectly since the industry is highly user driven. Rides are often custom made
Network involves public policy /actors?	Yes	No	No

Table 7.3   Case studies in 'Human Health Care and Food'

Case no.	9	10	11	12	13
KIE phase	Product development and company foundation	Founding; development; effects and performance	Public policy iniatives for innovative food	Founding; development	Managing and performance
Focus	Interaction between an electronics spin-off and the textile sector	Development of network relationships	Collaborative research as a way to renew low-tech industry	Financing and development of KIE	Internationalization strategies
Industry	Medical devices	Medical devices	Agriculture and food industry	Life science	Gene sequencing and bioinformatics
Founding date	1999	1985–2005	1998–2008	1999	1999; reincorporated 2007
Number of employees	9	25 in 1999; 100 in 2002; 200 in 2010	66 projects studied	Starting with 6 partners to a maximum of over 130 back to 0	Founding:8 in 2007: about 100 in 2010: 1500 in China in 2011; 3800 in the world
Geographical area	Southern Europe	Europe	Europe	Asia-Australia	China
Main product	ECG T-shirt	Bone-anchored hearing aids	Renewal in food industry, ranging from packaging to products to tests	IRI – a proteomics analysis instrument	Sequencing; testing; software development; health service and other
Network involves universities?	Yes	Yes	Yes	Yes	Yes
Network involves customers?	Yes	Yes	Yes	Yes	Yes
Network involves public policy /actors?	Yes	Yes	Yes	Yes	Yes

The 13 case studies in the companion book demonstrate how individual entrepreneurs and organizations deal with the three issues of balancing between business planning and uncertainty, stimulation of KIE ventures and how KIE ventures interact with the external environment. There are always major tensions between planning, carrying out those plans and finding new ways forward for the KIE venture.

The first issue is the balancing, and trade-offs, between planning and dealing with uncertainty. This also relates back to a long-standing debate within social sciences about the extent to which we have control over our environment and can make predictions about the future compared with the extent to which vital aspects are not under control but can occur unexpectedly and have unexpected consequences. This viewpoint matters when designing and evaluating public policy because we are arguing that you cannot just assume that the introduction of a policy instrument will 'automatically' have the desired effects.

Planning is the type of thinking that is already well represented in books and courses about entrepreneurship. Indeed, research results also indicate that companies need to apply more solid and systematic knowledge about the whole category of KIE ventures in order to develop decision-trees and choices. Thus, starting a company is partly based upon rational processes of planning, which help define goals, means and objectives.

Despite the intrinsic values of planning for the future, writing a business plan is not enough to start a company. Entrepreneurship is more about the complexity and long-term goals than the specific impact of planning per se.

Entrepreneurship involves uncertainty about the future, and therefore may also involve instances of something that 'just happens'. The founders and later managers often think one thing, end up somewhere else and have to adapt in the middle. This is demonstrated in the case study 'How tensions between exploration and exploitation drives the development process of KIE: the case of Sensor Inc.' (Lassen, 2013). Sensor Inc. is initially heavily reliant upon specialist technological knowledge, and gradually moves into production and sales. This move requires changes in strategy, management practices, human resources, network collaborations and financing sources alike. In bringing together these elements, the firm needs to manage and address the tensions between exploration of new ideas and exploitation of existing assets.

Thus, we can say that starting a KIE venture includes known elements as well as uncertainties. As illustrated in *How Entrepreneurs Do What They Do*, in many cases, these firms do not know if their technology will work, if customers will purchase, if they can access the many resources needed to achieve their goals and whether those resources will be internally obtained or externally through networks. These case studies all address this issue in different ways, and they can be called different types of uncertainty, such as technological uncertainty and market uncertainty. Will the technology work? Will the design be considered attractive? Are there any buyers and what are they looking for?

But uncertainty must be addressed, and decisions made. The founder and managers are decision-makers, and they must decide among alternative ways of solving technical problems, formation of markets and alternative uses or applications of their ideas for someone. These uncertainties tend to become visible after a time, or what is known as emergent.

Perhaps a unique characteristic – as compared to entrepreneurship in general – is the degree of uncertainty and risk-taking. Many KIE ventures at some point in their development face a situation where a high degree of uncertainty exists about the future. In these types of entrepreneurial and innovation processes, decision-makers are making decisions, but with little – or unreliable – information about future possible risks and rewards.

The second issue is how the linkages between firm and the external environment affect opportunities and knowledge for the KIE venture. There are practical implications too. By understanding that balance, or the struggle between the internal and external perspectives, you will have a better chance of succeeding with the KIE venture and designing appropriate public policy goals and instruments.

Practical stories such as those found in the 13 case studies as well as general research results show that there is a balance between how and why the KIE venture makes its own internal decisions compared to external influences. Basically, the key issue is how much the KIE management decisions affect its success or failure as opposed to the influences of external actors and processes which can also have positive, or negative, effects on the KIE venture.

Let us think about opportunities and knowledge, and how they are created. Both opportunities and knowledge are partly something created inside the firm, and partly something co-created with stakeholders like customers, government agencies and so on. The case study 'Entrepreneurial exploitation of creative destruction and the ambiguity of knowledge in the emerging field of digital advertising' (Broberg et al., 2013) follows individuals as they move between organizations and develop this creative new thing, later called digital advertising. In this case, KIE in service firms is affected by the fact that knowledge is an uncertain asset, and so the chapter explores how ambiguity often arises in terms of technology, business and market potentials.

Designing opportunities through knowledge requires that an individual founder (or founding team) can identify, mobilize and exploit innovative opportunities (Holmén et al., 2007). This means that some organizations may be better prepared and able than others to understand how the market is developing, which technologies are relevant and how to translate these competencies into successful business models. The dilemma for the policy-maker may be to decide whether to stimulate all KIE ventures or only those with a good chance of succeeding. Theoretically, the perspective here translates into an understanding of why certain KIE ventures are better than others at identifying relevant market and technological opportunities and turning those opportunities into profit-making ventures.

For public policy, a key arena to affect KIE in recent years has been at the regional level. The quality and type of knowledge that is available regionally or within one industry may have an impact upon the success, or failure, of later spin-offs. An example of this is found in the case study 'Knowledge intensive entrepreneurship from firm exit in a high-tech cluster: the case of the wireless communications cluster in Aalborg, Denmark' (Østergaard and Park, 2013). Large global firms pull out of a region due to the global crisis, and the chapter traces how certain individuals leave that firm, but remain in the region and develop new start-ups. Knowledge may thus diffuse to other industrial sectors and into new organizations like start-ups through labour mobility.

The third issue is which types of organizations matter for KIE. Let us state what we do not argue. This book has not argued that academic spin-offs are the only form for KIE. Nor does the evidence support the notion that academic spin-offs would be better positioned to commercialize ideas. This book has not argued that all KIE ventures lead to small firms, or spin-offs, but we have instead noted that additional organizational forms exist.

KIE can also have aims other than profit motives, which is captured in concepts like frugal innovation and social entrepreneurship. These types of phenomena and processes are generally organized through NGOs or communities. They may also lead to the start-up of KIE ventures and interactions between communities, NGOs, start-ups and large global companies.

Primarily, we have been interested in KIE ventures and have thought about small companies. One reason is that KIE will be useful in addressing 'wicked problems' or grand societal challenges, and KIE ventures are one powerful organizational solution in bringing together people, resources and ideas.

In addition to KIE ventures per se, KIE may also occur through other organizational solutions as well as aims other than profit. Examples include large companies that innovate. This type of entrepreneurship can help introduce and stimulate dynamics in existing firms and sectors, often through novel technologies commercialized through a venture. An example of this can be found in the chapter 'Collaborative research in innovative food: an example of renewing a traditional low-tech sector' (McKelvey et al., 2013). Public policy initiatives for collaborative research between large firms, KIE ventures and universities were designed to stimulate the development of a series of related products, competencies, specific technologies, instruments and measuring techniques.

7.3   ACCESSING RESOURCES AND IDEAS

This section addresses societal impacts and public policy related to variables for accessing resources and ideas. It represents an early phase for KIE ventures, but also one that lasts during the firm start-up, as an interactive process involving designing and choosing the inputs needed. Four issues are addressed, following the discussion in Chapter 3, namely sources of knowledge inputs; characteristics and traits of founders; financing, and societal influences.

7.3.1   Sources of Knowledge Inputs

The first topic is the sources of knowledge inputs. The literature about sources and endowments into KIE ventures has primarily been analysed through larger datasets, focused upon either technology-based firms, academic spin-offs or corporate spin-offs.

In order to understand the scope of public policy and societal impacts, more details are needed to design specific policies, as they will be limited by existing elements such as the existence of universities and large firms. The results, which are discussed in more detail below, suggest that public policy may need to obtain more distinct tools and analyse the similarities and differences between academic spin-offs and corporate spin-offs.

These two types of ventures clearly differ in terms of rationale for starting, the impacts, the rates of growth and relationship between parent firm and spin-off. Firm formation may be determined by aspects that are not under the control of the entrepreneur but may be amenable to other forms of societal impact, such as how to form the relationships between the parent organization(s) and KIE venture or the pull out of a region previously dominated by a large industrial concentration may stimulate corporate spin-offs.

One aspect is that the university might impact society by transferring entrepreneurial know-how via training and by facilitating new venture team formation (providing an important social context). The evidence on university spin-offs suggests a variety of ways in which universities contribute to new ventures. Initially, the focus has been upon those academic spin-offs started by researchers at the university. But the role of the university in stimulating KIE ventures can be much greater than that, especially through the role of students and alumni. Different impacts might be achieved by creating linkages to older alumni possibly through entrepreneurial networks (for example, regional alumni clubs).

The reason for the diverse impacts has to do with the fact that the university represents an organization dedicated to developing and diffusing different types of knowledge (McKelvey and Holmèn, 2006; Deiaco et al., 2012). Universities do so through education and teaching as well as community service and third stream activities. The people appear to be the main carriers of knowledge in these studies. The university also impacts societal well-being and economic growth through many other forms of technology transfer. Likely the most important mechanism is the movement of people due to the need to apply knowledge to new problem sets, requiring a creative further development of knowledge for a specific area of industrial application.

As with the university spin-offs, the evidence on corporate spin-offs suggests that there are many ways in which existing corporations may engage in and also impact new ventures. Corporate venturing primarily takes place in larger companies with significant R&D resources. The rationale is to make money out of ideas that would otherwise never be exploited as opportunities in the company. This means that the founder would move from the parent organization to the new venture.

A key issue for KIE and how to stimulate it is: What is then taken along? Knowledge, resources, networks and similar interactions between the founder and venture with the external environment represent more than a knowledge spill-over mechanism as the transfer is directed, specific and time-limited. Key aspects that facilitate a positive impact on the new venture include the complementarity of the resource base of the parent firm relative to its spin-off, the intensity of collaboration between the parent and the spin-off, and the dependence of the spin-off firm on the resources provided by the parent organization. Thus, much richer taxonomies of different types of spin-offs can be developed, and each one may have differential impacts upon firm growth and performance.

7.3.2 Characteristics and Traits of Founders

The second topic relates to the characteristics and traits of founders. One implication for public policy is how to stimulate an entrepreneurial mindset, especially in relation to the topics of cognition, risk and 'over-trust' in own abilities.

One could further strengthen a current focus of relevant policy, namely educating people, to obtain a more entrepreneurial mindset and skills. But a key problem is the chicken and egg dilemma – do you need entrepreneurs to first be interested in starting a company and then obtain skills, or vice versa? By this, we mean that the literature does not determine whether founders' perceived competence in entrepreneurial, managerial and technical roles developed before or concurrent with their founding of successful businesses. To answer this question, longitudinal research and coherent databases over a longer time period are needed to determine which comes first, as well as the extent to which they are interlinked.

Of course, these characteristics and traits are in one sense positive and help start companies. Certainly, many new ventures that later become successful probably would not have been started without these cognitive biases of the founder(s).

At the same time, there are negative aspects. Many of these ventures will fail and, indeed, many of the cognitive biases can cause an entrepreneur to underestimate the amount of risk associated with a particular venture. On the system level, failures are part of the phenomena of entrepreneurship, and yet these failures may also be seen as wasting resources.

This fact then raises two questions for designing and evaluating public policy in relation to societal impacts. One is whether society wishes to stimulate more risk-taking behaviour and overly optimistic assessments of the business prospects, given the finding that entrepreneurs tend to make incorrect assumptions, being too positive about possible outcomes and underestimating the likelihood of failure. Stimulating entrepreneurial behavior is necessary for society – but the individuals may have unrealistic goals and expectations, leading to large risks of failure. Another is a more limited view, where public policy ought to focus upon only stimulating entrepreneurship when it is 'likely' to be successful. Developing this type of policy further would require us to examine in more depth the nature of the relationship between one's possession of human capital (like education) and access to resources or social capital relevant for entrepreneurship.

Another way to look at this is that there are several moderating factors, which seem to play into this discussion of cognition, risk and over-trust. These moderating factors work out in ways that suggest that societal impacts can be stimulated and conceptualized as impacts on other variables. For example, improving the type of information search and developing a more adaptive business plan can help stimulate success. In this way, one could further lead aside the question of whether the entrepreneurs' risk perceptions are accurate or not, to instead see how the moderating influences affect the relationship between these accurate risk perceptions and new venture success.

Additionally, psychological factors (for example, personal efficacy, need for achievement and locus of control) and demographic factors (for example, age, entrepreneurial parents and education) could be incorporated into predictions of entrepreneurial behaviour, and the success of the venture. The issue becomes whether the results are 'believable' enough to make valid recommendations, such as using psychological tests to determine which individuals are predicted to perform. By focusing upon these moderating factors, changes may then encourage an entrepreneurial mindset, but do so by slightly shifting the mix between risk perception and exploitation of opportunities.

Finally, a potentially powerful policy goal could be to stimulate or increase the likelihood of serial entrepreneurship, that is, the launching of multiple ventures by the same entrepreneur. This would enable the beneficial effect of knowledge spill-overs across a portfolio of start-ups. There are advantages and disadvantages to focusing public policy on serial entrepreneurs as well but they represent one way forward. The advantage could be to strengthen the formation and performance of the ventures. The disadvantage could be that those already in the game are strengthened whereas the inexperienced entrepreneurs wishing to start up might not receive help, thereby further exasperating unevenness of development.

Indeed, what matters about the characteristics and traits of founders is that many of these characteristics and traits reported as important are related to the acquisition of knowledge and its application in a business setting. This implies that the potential founder can improve the chances of engaging in KIE through developing skills, experience, education and networks that influence both the knowledge and the commercialization aspects. For example, he or she can be active in acquiring technological and scientific knowledge through education; they can develop networks and social capital with either entrepreneurs or relevant user companies; and they can learn about markets from potential customers.

7.3.3 Financing

The third topic is financing. In the evidence about sources and types of capital it is clear that venture capital is only one of multiple financing sources, perhaps especially for KIE compared to large firms and entrepreneurship in general. KIE ventures tend to be financed by the individual and their families.

An implication for public policy is that venture capital is only one of many financing sources for the formation of companies reliant upon knowledge. Some types of financing are important to the firms, but likely organized outside the market, such as family or personal savings and the intervention of business angels. Some types of financing are given by large corporations, usually ones highly dependent upon R&D, and they are used as a way to manage the spin-off activities of the large companies. Other types of financing are public, where complementary policy instruments like incubators can affect the performance of firms. This implies that public policy needs to differentiate different types and sources of financing, and also address the interactions amongst different domains of policy.

In thinking about these issues, we note that KIE ventures share particular characteristics that limit their options for obtaining financing from external sources. These characteristics include: they have little or no collateral; their assets tend to be intangible; and the value of their innovation is hard to calculate. For these reasons, entrepreneurs that rely upon a more knowledge intensive approach – regardless of the sector – tend to rely largely on equity financing. Another result is that previous experience (for example, experiential) and the knowledge base of the founder as well as relational capital in networks affect the types and amounts of capital available to a new venture. The founders also tend to spread risks so that they are not overly dependent upon one source.

Another implication for public policy is the potentially interesting role of the large corporation. Chapter 3 particularly focused upon the managed spin-off (corporate venture or CVC) as related to tools for financing. The relationship between the parent company and the corporate spin-off also continues to affect the venture later during the management and development phase, including aspects related to leverage and profitability.

Interestingly, though, there is more to be examined as to why technological diversity does not seem to moderate the relationship between CVC investments and innovation. An important issue is whether these corporate spin-offs tend to be concentrated in the same industries as the large firms because they represent internal projects or whether corporate investor firms search broadly outside the firm for ideas. This also suggests an uneven development, whereby regions with highly educated and/or R&D intensive large corporations may be able to stimulate spin-offs but regions lacking this type of enterprise structure cannot do so.

The evidence on corporate venturing suggests that large firms with a high R&D intensity or educated labour can offer an alternative route to obtain financing for primarily managed corporate spin-outs. The ideas for these ventures were likely developed in the R&D labs of the parent companies, or in highly educated pools of people working in service environments, so that many major investments into the knowledge base have already been made.

A final implication for public policy is the role of mechanisms and regulations that affect the ability of companies to survive and change over time. Financing is not a one-off need of the company. Obtaining new and repeated sources of financing may be related to organizational changes that affects whether the firm continues to exist, and in what ways, later on. For example, the firm may move from private equity to being publically traded through an IPO, or be bought up by a larger company. The entrance and exit of the venture per se may involve many steps, even if the idea, technology and product remains the same (or similar) over longer periods of time. Hence, there may be the need to stimulate intermediary policy goals, such as reviewing regulatory conditions for buy-outs or bankruptcy.

7.3.4　Societal Influences and Public Policy

The final topic is related to societal influences. The evidence about the impacts of financing and public policy on high-tech clusters is mixed. On the one hand, public policy can obviously play a role in stimulating new enterprises and possibly also high-tech clusters in specific regions. There are then debates about whether the market allocates optimally and therefore public policy by definition gives financing to the most efficient firms, and will choose from the weaker remaining firms. By mimicking the market, this first view is that public policy can over-invest and under-invest at the wrong time, or invest in weaker enterprises (that could not obtain financing on the market). However, it may be the function of public policy, though, to identify marginal technologies and products, or ones in less favourable regions, and give them a chance. That is the other side of the debate, related to a different view of the need for policy in an imperfect system.

An interesting aspect may be the possibility that public policy can interact with venture capital in order to spread new venture creation to regions and technologies that are not favoured in the market. This raises many difficult questions about whether public policy should try to 'even out' the fact that financing is unevenly distributed geographically and sectorally, or not.

The answers to these types of questions depend partly on whether the goals of policy are to stimulate societal well-being and economic growth throughout society or whether the goals are to stimulate the new enterprises that are the most likely to lead to rapid growth. This is related to the previous section, in that financing is a key area in which public policy goals and instruments have been focused upon stimulating and supporting KIE ventures.

A key result for policy is to harmonize or at least relate and discuss the impact and goals of different types of policy. For example, policy to support an already functioning science park may help promote customer contacts, while firms outside a cluster or strong region may need help to better balance local and international contacts. Policy should not give priority *a priori* to one type of geographical relationship, for example, local, national or international.

7.4   MANAGING AND DEVELOPING THE KIE VENTURE

This section addresses societal impacts related to the processes of managing and developing a KIE venture. This phase often requires a reconfiguration of resources and ideas in order to bring the strategic vision and organizational structure in line with market potentials. This includes: human resources; networks, growth patterns; and internationalization.

7.4.1   Human Resources

The topic of human resources, including human capital more broadly, is clearly relevant for KIE, given that the findings suggest that individuals with experience and education can start and grow new ventures. This suggests that public policy can play a strong role, as entrepreneurs are 'created' rather than 'just existing' in society. One avenue may be labour mobility, especially encouraging a swap of jobs across creative people, people working in industry or academia. The reason is that many of the studies suggest that previous work experience is vital for later perform-ance of high-tech ventures, as well as bringing new ideas into the low-tech sector and services. Another avenue is to focus upon mechan-isms that increase the knowledge intensity of existing companies through technology transfer – such as consultancy or working with universities to develop innovations – rather than the formation of ventures per se.

7.4.2 Networks

Policy instruments in later stages of the venture development may need to stress the network per se, rather than the individuals. In literature on networks the interaction leading to and exploiting social capital tends to take place between individuals – rather than between firms or organ-izations. Therefore, the founder and the founding team are essential concepts. The literature suggests that it is the founder who builds networks with other team members and with external agents.

An important empirical finding from the reported research is that social capital, and related networks, play an important role for the knowledge intensive entrepreneurial process. Networks are involved in multiple ways. First, the social capital is helpful in establishing the business venture, for example, by creating a functioning founding team and raising the required start-up capital. Second, in the further develop-ment of the firm the social capital enables the founders to gain access to needed resources, such as new capital and employees. Social capital also enhances the credibility of the venture firm and facilitates identification of market opportunities, and can compensate even in the short run for the lack of economic capital.

We would encourage analysis of policy instruments to differentiate the types of alliances needed. In biotechnology, exemplifying a science-based industry, strategic alliances and linkages are important to the small venture firms, both in relation to universities and large industrial com-panies such as ones in pharmaceuticals. But the reason for interacting with them differs. University collaborations are critical for enhancing credibility and reputation while inter-firm collaborations are critical for product development and commercialization.

7.4.3 Growth Patterns

The research suggests that public policy may need to further distinguish the needs and demands of large firms compared to small firms, but also develop new policy instruments and goals that stimulate interaction or learning across different types of organizations. Small firms are usually associated with simple processes and management systems. However, this book provides evidence to the contrary. Small KIE ventures are not simple, and learning and adaptation is needed as well as a planning philosophy. A key result is that promoting a philosophy of leadership that is more focused upon planning, and upon more systematic evaluation of the internal assets of the KIE may prove useful in promoting growth. At the same time, the literature provides some caution in assuming system-wide characteristics can explain differences in the dynamics of the firms given the continuing importance of the characteristics of the individuals involved, as well as the organization as a whole.

Thus, growth patterns of KIE are interesting and especially the need for management (and managers) in both ventures and established companies to balance the requirements and demands of larger, stable, resource-driven management styles with those of smaller, flexible, opportunity-driven management styles. This implies that although there are significant differences in the types of management, public policy could through education support both types.

One main issue for public policy is how to develop instruments to promote entrepreneurial learning. A clear issue is the need to develop learning not only about technological knowledge but also, or even especially, market knowledge, such as the demands of customers. Feed-back loops in which groups of entrepreneurs learn from each other could also be promoted. What is clear is that entrepreneurial learning as related to knowledge acquisition does not rely on hands-off market relationships but instead on other types of social relationships.

Other interesting evidence for public policy is the value of planning – despite earlier remarks about balancing planning with uncertainty. Given the evidence unearthed about the value of planning, future evaluation of public policy impacts upon new ventures should examine the relative importance of planning as a process and plans as an outcome. One specific topic to examine is the effects of the amount of time spent on business planning because this factor could have a non-monotonic relationship with disbanding, firm organizing activity and product development in new ventures.

Another area relates to training. Assuming that new venture success depends on both personal commitment and a viable market opportunity, entrepreneurship training might be used to enhance a potential entrepreneur's strengths with complementary skills and knowledge. Hence, training that recognizes the different reasons why successful entrepreneurs are willing to persist in entrepreneurial activity is a potentially interesting venue to pursue when identifying and training potential students. Knowledge about providing services and markets (and marketing) are important, as well as the more usually discussed technological and scientific knowledge.

This transition from a focus upon exploration to exploitation in the market has perhaps been understood for many years in more general terms, but the policy instruments have been fairly blunt. It is difficult for policy to intervene in order to promote a more market-oriented and less technology-oriented perspective for the firm. Still, one could interpret some existing policy instruments in these terms, such as subsidies for demonstration projects or soft loans for products to be introduced into markets. These types of policy instruments try to provide incentives and resources for firms that are more oriented towards the market, and market opportunities.

Traditionally, this dichotomy is associated with quite a few challenges found at the core of the definition of KIE. The key issue is particularly how to balance between a focus on knowledge intensive development and a focus on bringing the knowledge efficiently to market in terms of product, processes or services, and thereby creating wealth. If policy can provide or facilitate things like demonstration projects, collaborative product development, networks and other experiences of trust in purchasing and working with new firms, then this may help mediate the information and trust gaps that new firms face.

7.4.4 Internationalization

The relationship between the development of the venture and internationalization is relevant given the global nature of the modern economy. The KIE service firms appear to be more immediately focused upon internationalization, suggesting that their market is global rather than local. They may need specific support structures, such as access to networks that can help identify possible collaborators (and competitors) needed to supply international goods and services. On the flip side, public policy that primarily focuses upon regional networks and relationships may be counterproductive for these types of firms.

7.5 EVALUATING PERFORMANCE

This section moves to evaluating performance, and our argument is the need for a more nuanced and careful understanding of what evaluating performance – and evaluating the impacts of public policy – may entail. Simple measures of 'academic entrepreneurship' as patents or academic spin-offs may be tempting – but also provide incorrect information about underlying processes of KIE.

The research outlined in Chapters 3 to 5 suggests that the process of new firm formation is more complex than previously imagined. For university academics, it is not just an issue of the individual starting a company but also a question of whether and what types of resources and support they obtain from other organizations. Corporate governance mechanisms have also been shown to be similarly diverse, with different impacts upon the actual management and strategy of the firm. This suggests that both academic spin-offs and corporate spin-offs are likely to be unevenly distributed, with the highest concentration in areas where they receive relevant support.

These results also suggest that policy may need different measures of what constitutes a high level of firm formation in different regions or different types of technologies. Indeed, certain foci of previous policy may simply be wrong.

A key area of public policy in recent decades has been the need to stimulate patenting and IPR, especially ones related to universities and academics. Some of this policy push, particularly in Europe, has been related to an assumption that countries lag behind the USA. However, we also know that many KIE ventures do not hold patents but instead use other means to protect their knowledge and innovations. We suggest that public policy shifts its focus to a more modern view of knowledge assets in the firm.

Firm formation is a key indicator often used to assess and evaluate the impact of public policy. As such, the proxy is often taken as given, for example, as a useful and relevant measure of the impact of policy upon entrepreneurship. However, public policy needs to keep in mind both the expected effects of growth and performance as well as the expected timeline. As illustrated throughout this book as well as the companion book *How Entrepreneurs Do What They Do*, KIE ventures tend to grow and shrink rapidly, and this is often dependent upon the external financing obtained and/or introduction of viable products and services. Understanding such dynamics is important when evaluating the impact of public policy because many effects may take a long time and the performance may vary widely in different time periods.

7.6 IN CONCLUSION

In understanding the impacts on society and public policy for performance, we would like to end with some words on interpreting what these
entrepreneurs do.

Throughout our analysis, we have identified how in most knowledge
intensive ventures the entrepreneurs have become 'knowledge operators'
who work at the intersection between science, technology, creativity,
design, innovation and markets. Stimulating activity in this intersection
should therefore be the primary focus of public policy. These operators –
whether start-up companies, established corporations or academic institutions – engage in KIE in any of three ways: they utilize existing
knowledge; they combine different knowledge assets; and they create
new knowledge. Many successful entrepreneurs do all three.

The biggest challenge for them, however, is often in moving between
the focus upon the 'idea', known as the innovative opportunity, and the
'product and service', that is, ways to make returns and appropriate the
returns to their investment on the market – or through public contracts.

One mistake is that public policy is still largely concerned with product
innovation and firms that rely upon advanced technology in high-tech
industries or university spin-offs in relation to KIE. This research
suggests that this knowledge creation provides a type of public good
relevant to many other actors within the economy. The KIE firms are
reliant upon others in their network, but they may also provide knowledge resources useful for others. Hence, in terms of analysing impacts, it
may be useful to take a broader view of impact and importance, and not
just focus upon immediate, obvious and measurable outputs. Moreover,
we must better understand the dynamics of low-tech sectors and services,
which rely upon other types of creative knowledge.

Appendix

A.1 INTRODUCTION

This appendix includes a detailed overview of the methodology for the initial literature review carried out to investigate what evidence has been generated on the topic of KIE. The review was based on previous concepts and keywords to develop an evidence-based approach to understanding KIE.

We would like to stress that although this appendix is restricted to the literature review, this book rests upon a novel conceptualization by the authors as synthesized in the chapters and KIE creation model. The conceptual framework and the KIE creation model can be seen as resulting from a systematic way of working to try to explain what we know about the world around us – as opposed to speculation, individual interpretations and the like. Therefore, we can generate knowledge about the phenomena, drawing from case studies as well as quantitative data. We have synthesized and condensed this in order to be able to say more about the processes, variables and outcomes of KIE ventures seen as a business proposition.

This appendix only focuses upon the underlying literature review. This book – and the companion case study book – also grew out of previous work. An initial review (Lassen et al., 2012) was a deliverable into the EU project called AEGIS, details of which can be found at http://www.aegis-fp7.eu. The objectives of that review paper were to: (1) identify contributions already made on the topic of KIE in different areas of research, through a systematic literature review; (2) define the concepts and empirical indicators and evidence used for each contribution; (3) develop the outline of the conceptual model integrating several aspects of current understandings; and (4) discuss the implications for public policy. This appendix reproduces some of the review tables, which highlight the foci of existing empirical and theoretical studies.

This appendix goes through in detail the methodology used for our systematic literature review, which also provides useful steps for others. We present the methodology because we stress that the book uses an evidence-based approach to learning about, engaging in and evaluating this type of entrepreneurship. This means that a substantial amount of scientific results have been condensed and synthesized here. The reason we point this out is that scientific results about KIE ventures and this type of entrepreneurship, as generally reported in this book, are based upon a vast body of knowledge.

Chapter 1 introduced the idea that the entrepreneur and the reader interested in starting a firm will have to balance 'doing' and 'knowing'. By 'doing' we mean engaging practically in actual venture creation processes, and by illustrations. By 'knowing' we mean learning through specific empirical examples and case studies as well as general knowledge and tools for evaluating processes and outcomes.

We provide a methodology based upon our experience, but outlining a more general way of working. Hence, our process describes the phases and steps needed in order to assess the state-of-the-art literature, or 'knowing', as this may be helpful for scholars, including students writing a thesis.

The first phase is the methodology for the systematic review of the existing literature. The second phase is synthesis and conceptualization. And the background of where we started is relevant to understand where this might be useful. No literature review existed that captured what we wanted to study. The first phase was obviously necessary. A solid foundation of existing literature was also necessary if we were to make sense of which variables and phases were key for KIE in the second phase.

A.2 PHASE I: METHODOLOGY FOR SYSTEMATIC LITERATURE REVIEW

This section describes Phase I, which we call a methodology for the systematic review of the existing literature. We had a particular starting point. We knew that many articles existed, and that different results could be found in the existing literature – and for related phenomena. This had previously been studied in many different disciplines and journals. But we also knew that KIE was previously not an accepted concept, with a given definition, that could be easily found.

Within this phase, we present four major steps that are general for others wishing to replicate this methodology. We set up a four-step process for a systematic literature review as illustrated in Figure A.1.[1]

Step 1 consists of defining the criteria for the search. This includes inclusion criteria and exclusion criteria. Step 2 consists of identifying the key words. These can be ones already found in the literature known to

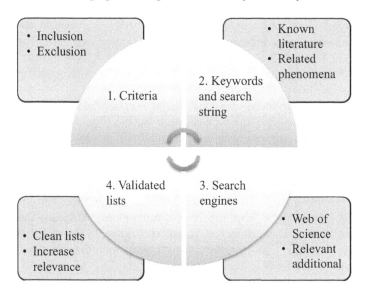

Figure A.1   Phase I: four steps for a systematic literature review

the authors, or can be concepts and variable found in related phenomena. Step 3 requires the choice of search engines. Web of Science is a given, and there are usually relevant additional search engines. Step 4 relates to developing the validated lists. This leads to a descriptive analysis of the existing literature.

We shall also describe our specific case in relation to each step. This is to help the understanding of the flow of work and choices to be made.

We would also like to point out that the undertaking was a team effort. Other members of the team were given smaller tasks to complete while McKelvey and Lassen structured, synthesized and interpreted the results. The work was carried out at the Institute of Innovation and Entre-preneurship, University of Gothenburg, and by colleagues at the Institute of Management Innovation and Technology linked to other universities, who were conducting the study of KIE.

A.2.1   Step 1: Criteria for the Search

Step 1 consists of defining the criteria for the search. This includes inclusion criteria and exclusion criteria for finding and choosing articles. As an overall guideline, we recommend that authors establish both inclusion and exclusion criteria for defining the set of interesting research contributions.

This may seem straightforward, and in some cases such criteria are easy to identify. If the topic runs across several fields, or if similar concepts are used to describe essentially the same phenomena, however then the author needs to read a set of important articles first. For Master's thesis students, such articles are often proposed by the supervisor but they could also come from an independent search.

In all cases, it is very important that the author keeps track, and documents, exactly which choices are made. A key issue to ask is whether the study will focus upon articles relevant for the topic, which are well established, or whether the study will focus attention on not well-established concepts or topics of research.

Otherwise, if the writer does not keep track, then the literature review will have a type of selection bias in relation to the existing literature, meaning that only a limited part of the existing knowledge as found in the scientific literature is covered and the rest is ignored. Although selection bias is a term used for quantitative research, the thinking about only examining a sub-population of possible units is relevant to thinking about the existing literature. The reason is that there is usually a huge amount of literature on any given topic or research question, and the selection of some articles – and ignoring others – will lead to a focus on a narrow range.

Thus, to keep track of these choices, we recommend tables similar to Tables A.1 and A.2 on inclusion criteria and exclusion criteria. For each criterion, one must be able to explain the reasons made, and also link this to the actual choices made when reviewing the literature.

In our case, it was fairly complex. We could not just put 'knowledge intensive entrepreneurship' into the search engine and come up with a set of acceptable and relevant articles. Entrepreneurship as we wished to portray it is a complex process. We wanted to identify literature that was in high-tech sectors and low-tech sectors, as well as literature using qualitative methods, quantitative methods and mixed methods. There were some aids and short-cuts. We did know that some existing concepts had been used frequently to describe sub-sets of what we were trying to capture, such as the more limited concepts of 'academic spin-offs', 'technology-based firms' and 'high-tech start-ups'. So we could identify some key concepts previously used, but we also knew they were very narrow sub-sets of the larger phenomena and processes, as defined in this book. In our view, KIE is valuable because it provides a synthesis and novel concepts and models and thus provides a novel model as compared to existing constructs.

The inclusion criteria established a broad focus of the research in terms of time span, journals and topics of potential interest for the understanding of KIE. We agreed upon the seven criteria listed in Table A.1.

Table A.1   Criteria for inclusion in KIE review

No.	Criteria	Reason for inclusion
1	Theoretical papers	Identification of commonalities and differences in definitions applied. To be used for conceptualization.
2	All sectors/industries	To capture sector specificities and commonalities.
3	Quantitative and qualitative empirical studies	To capture all empirical evidence, and draw on the strengths of both paradigmatic approaches.
4	1980–2009	To capture the development of research on the topic.
5	Articles published in scientific journals	Peer-reviewed publications are considered to be the most valid.
6	Articles published in journals with scope within entrepreneurship, knowledge management and innovation management	Journals with main scope on topics outside these three fields may indeed have published articles on the topic of KIE. However, it is regarded as more valid for the purpose of this book that the articles reviewed are part of a clear stream of research.
7	The knowledge intensive venture as primary unit of analysis	The main unit of analysis for the AEGIS project.

The exclusion criteria set certain limitation for the research scope in terms of unit of analysis, fields of study and type of publications reviewed. This is beneficial for ensuring the coherence and validity of the review. We agreed upon five exlusion criteria listed in Table A.2.

We defined and discussed both the inclusion and exclusion criteria through discussions in a wider research group. We then distributed our results widely in the AEGIS project, consisting of 30 partners across Europe to identify mistakes and additional literature.

Table A.2   Criteria for exclusion in KIE review

No.	Criteria	Reason for exclusion
1	Pre-1980	Entrepreneurship as a field of research has mainly developed since the 1980s (with the exception of a number of seminal macroeconomic studies). Hence, most relevant articles will be published post-1980.
2	Macroeconomic effects	For the purpose of this study focus is placed on the intra- and inter-firm unit of analysis.
3	Working papers/ proceedings/reports etc.	Such work may be of interest, but has not been through a thorough review process and is hence excluded.
4	Non-English language	To avoid strong local/regional biases often associated with journals in national languages.
5	Internal corporate venturing	Focus of the review is on the establishment of new external ventures, hence not considering the aspects of internal rejuvenating activities.

A.2.2   Step 2: Key Search Words

Step 2 consists of identifying the key search words and search strings. These can be ones already found in the literature known to the authors or can be concepts and variables found in related phenomena.

The way that one defines key search words will influence the results. In other words, step 2 is the first in several steps aimed at the data selection and collection process. It should help to increase validity in the research results. 'Validity' is a concept generally reserved for empirical studies. However, we mean that it is also applicable for understanding whether all the relevant processes and variables are included in the search for literature.

Note that in most cases, especially students' theses, the aim is to define a narrow question that can be identified as unique and answered. In our case, we were developing a new, synthetic concept. Therefore, a wide set of key search words was desirable.

The concept of KIE may refer to a wide range of different aspects, hence research publications in diverse journals may be relevant to identify in order to further develop and conceptualize the area. We did some initial searches and reading and consulted experts (professors).

It became apparent that a very inclusive approach was needed in order to establish a representative set of keywords for identifying appropriate literature. The review team first identified keywords on the subject based on prior experience. Second, the generated list of keywords was verified through discussion and peer-review in the research team covering scholars in the fields of entrepreneurship, innovation management and knowledge management.

The final list included these keywords: academic spin-off; corporate spin-off; corporate venturing; high-tech entrepreneurship; knowledge-based entrepreneurship; knowledge intensive entrepreneurship; knowledge intensive innovation; knowledge intensive start-up; knowledge intensive ventures; R&D and knowledge intensive; R&D and venturing; science intensive entrepreneurship; technology-based entrepreneurship; university spin-off; venture creation; venture creation and R&D.

A.2.3　Step 3: Search Engines

Step 3 requires the choice of search engines. Web of Science is a given, and there are usually relevant additional search engines. The question of which one to use will depend upon the field, and usually a senior scholar or the librarian can help identify relevant search engines.

For our study, we chose two search engines for scientific articles. The keywords were used in two major search engines, Web of Science and EBSCO. We tried several search engines and came to the following conclusions.

The search engines were selected based on their complementary strengths.

- Web of Science has particular strengths when it comes to identifying research on KIE especially, but not exclusively, related to technological aspects and industries.
- EBSCO has particular strengths when it comes to identifying research on KIE especially, but not exclusively, related to socio-economic and management aspects.

In our case, a total of 1044 distinct citations were identified based on the initial keyword search. By distinct citations, we mean distinct author-article pairs identified in the databases.

A.2.4 Step 4: Validated Lists

Step 4 relates to developing the validated lists. This leads to a descriptive analysis of the existing literature.

This step requires a lot of effort and manual examination of the literature. This is one reason why students' theses should be more limited in topic and scope, and should relate to an existing concept and theory that can be found in the literature.

The detailed information of how we worked should be useful for others to set up their own process and stages. By 'citations' below we mean what we hope will turn out to be full papers, consisting of author-article pairs. But it was not obvious that even the best search engines work well or turn up relevant articles, and therefore the basis of scholarship – reading and evaluating – is key in this step.

The research team was able to do the following steps to increase validity:

1. The total sample of citations was reviewed manually to exclude obvious misfits. Such misfits included, for example, doubles of citations due to classification errors, incomplete citations and citations clearly off topic. This reduced the sample to 997 citations.
2. Next, the citations identified were reviewed according to the inclusion/exclusion criteria. This reduced the total number of citations to 386.
3. This reduced list of citations was presented to a number of scholars in the fields of entrepreneurship, innovation management and knowledge management. They were asked as experts in the field. This was done in order to verify the list; the experts were asked to add or delete citations based on their professional recommendations. The list was reduced by 11 citations, and three were added, making the total 378.
4. Hereafter, the validated list was sorted into what we defined as categories A, B and C by relevance. This was primarily done by reading abstracts and sometimes full papers. The A-list represented articles of particular relevance, the B-list represented articles of some interest and the C-list represented articles of more peripheral interest. The AEGIS research team (30 universities) was invited to review the A-list in order to determine if the scope of the articles included was satisfactory.
5. The A-list, consisting of 142 articles, was considered the main sample as these were of high interest and relevance.
6. The 142 articles on the A-list were further scrutinized. Upon initial

review of the A-list articles it became apparent that a number of articles were published in journals without a clear focus on topics related to KIE. We wished to exclude papers with keywords but without substance to our phenomena.

7.   Hence, journals with only one publication in the A-list sample were excluded. The final validated A-list includes 106 articles (Table A.3).

Table A.3   Journals included

Journal	No. of published articles
Journal of Business Venturing	15
Entrepreneurship Theory and Practice	12
Technovation	11
Research Policy	9
European Planning Studies	7
Small Business Economics	7
International Journal of Technology Management	6
International Small Business Journal	6
Technology Analysis and Strategic Management	5
R&D Management	4
Science and Public Policy	4
Strategic Management Journal	4
Academy of Management Review	3
Research-Technology Management	3
California Management Review	2
Journal of Business	2
Journal of Business Research	2
Journal of Small Business Management	2
Research Evaluation	2
Total	106

The list was examined by the research team again. We concluded that the list adequately included articles covering topics on entrepreneurship which are well-known and well cited, as well as articles that address topics which have been researched to a lower degree but represented important results for our review.

A.3 PHASE II: SYNTHESIS AND CONCEPTUALIZATION

This section describes Phase II, which is a more active step of research. The existing research needs to be turned into a framework of understanding that is useful. It could be useful in the sense of setting up a list of variables that will be used to ask questions in interviews, or in the sense of setting up a model of causality that can be tested quantitatively, or in the sense of developing a conceptual framework linking different things.

We identify four main steps (Figure A.2), which we outline below to facilitate others wishing to replicate this methodology. We provide information about our case as well, although in this case, the results are more easily found in all the previous chapters in this book. Therefore, the description here is quite short.

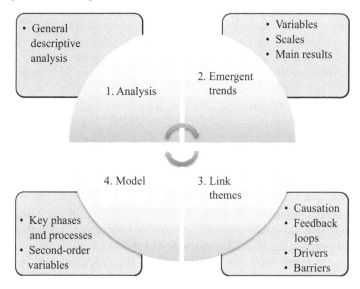

Figure A.2   Phase II: four steps in synthesis and conceptualization

Step 1 consists of analysis of the results of Phase I. A key issue is to identify a general descriptive analysis of the state-of-the-art literature. Exactly how this looks depends upon the ambition level, aim of the research and the topic. There are issues related to whether the research has a quantitative or qualitative approach, as well as understanding the research design and methodology.

Step 2 consists of identifying emergent themes that were identified. Key aspects to consider are:

- for quantitative studies, the independent and dependent variables
- scales and indicators
- databases
- main results.

Some of the results from Steps 1 and 2 are presented in the concluding section below.

Step 3 requires a more complex understanding so that one can generate and understand the interlinkages between the emerging themes. This relates to issues like causation, feedback loops and the drivers and barriers to change.

Step 4 relates to structuring the ideas into one model. This is based upon the processes, phases and interlinkages identified.

In our case, this leads to the comprehensive understanding of the key phases and second-order variables, which we developed into the KIE creation model. This was based upon a deeper theoretical understanding of the literature that also went beyond the processes and second-order variables per se to define our unique contributions. This included the development of the propositions that frame this book and each of the chapters.

A.4 DESCRIPTIVE ANALYSIS OF THE STATE OF THE ART

This section provides a descriptive state-of-the-art understanding of the literature that we could generate through our proposed methodology.

After performing Phase I and Phase II for KIE, we felt convinced that there is a great need for understanding this specific type of entrepreneurship. Moreover, we could identify many 'gaps' in the literature where it would be possible to contribute through novel research. The overview in relation to our conceptual model is shown in Figure A.3.

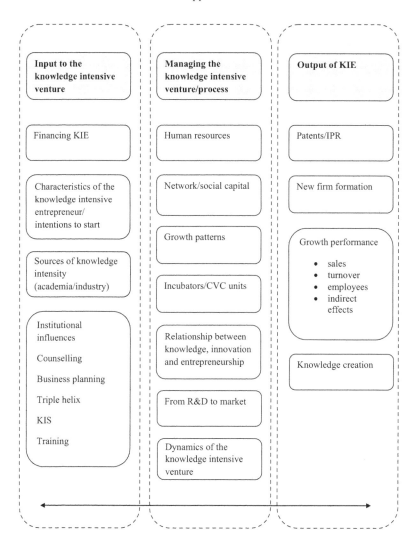

Figure A.3   Overview of conceptual elements

Three important points that we deduced from further examination of the literature are:

Point 1: Methodology for studies of KIE (Figure A.4, Table A.4)

- A relatively high focus on conceptual papers – the field is still unclearly positioned.
- A good mix between quantitative and qualitative studies but without a clear coherence between results from qualitative studies translated into quantitative research agendas.
- A lack of mixed-methods studies.

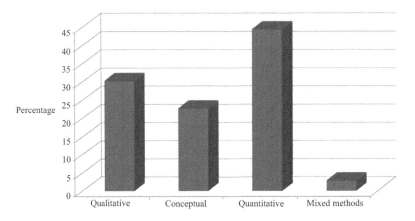

Figure A.4   Overview of methods used in KIE research

Point 2: Uneven distribution of KIE research focus (Figure A.5)

- The characteristics of entrepreneurs and how they finance their ventures are highly researched topics, while, for example, how entrepreneurs move from R&D to market focus or knowledge creation taking place through entrepreneurship are topics that are currently under-researched.

Table A.4   Overview of methods divided by main dimensions of KIE

Topics	Methods
Input to the knowledge intensive venture:	
• financing KIE	• 45% Quantitative
• characteristics of the knowledge intensive entrepreneur; intentions to start	• 29% Conceptual
	• 26% Qualitative
• sources of knowledge intensity (academia/industry)	• 0% Mixed methods
• institutional influences (counselling, business planning, triple helix, KIS, training)	
Managing the knowledge intensive venture/process:	
• human resources	• 38% Quantitative
• network/social capital	• 38% Qualitative
• growth patterns	• 19% Conceptual
• incubators/CVC units	• 6% Mixed methods
• relationship between knowledge, innovation and entrepreneurship	
• from R&D to market	
• dynamics of the knowledge intensive venture	
Output of KIE:	
• patents/IPR	• 73% Quantitative
• new firm formation	• 18% Conceptual
• growth performance (sales, turnover, employees, indirect effects)	• 9% Qualitative
	• 0% Mixed methods
• knowledge creation	

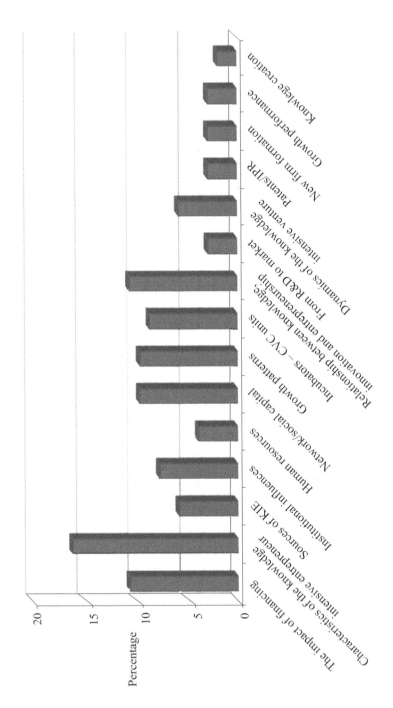

Figure A.5 Distribution of KIE research foci

Point 3: Limited understanding of KIE in different industrial settings

● Very little evidence is generated specifically on either low-tech industries or services.

Table A.5   KIE in low-tech, high-tech and service industries

Low-tech industry (traditional sector)	High-tech industry	Services
● innovativeness of organization ● application of knowledge intensive activities/ technologies in low-tech sectors ● complex practical knowledge (operational knowledge) ● high growth in low-growth sectors	● innovativeness of product/technology ● dynamics of knowledge intensive sectors ● R&D based ● science based	● innovativeness of business model ● public procurement of innovation

One of the specific challenges we concentrated on throughout the review is the definition of KIE, the variables connected to KIE and how KIE may be researched in a structured manner. The review has revealed a multitude of perspectives on KIE, which reflect the current unstructured nature of the field. While most studies of KIE focus on high-tech industries, the literature also demonstrates that KIE is a relevant aspect in a variety of different settings, high-tech, low-tech and services alike. As illustrated in Table A.5, we were able to pinpoint aspects of KIE pertaining to each of the three categories.

In this way the review allowed us to take several steps towards defining what KIE is and what KIE is not. This provided evidence that firms in low-tech sectors and in service sectors, as well as in high-tech sectors, are highly dependent upon different types of knowledge and combine that knowledge in order to explore and exploit opportunities. This suggests that KIE is a phenomena across the economy and across different types of firms, and not confined to certain sectors or certain types of spin-offs. Finally, the review also makes it possible to develop a coherent conceptual model of KIE, which integrates all aspects identified and organizes these according to the following phases: input variables;

management variables; and output variables. Positioning future studies of KIE clearly in relation to the variables described in the conceptual model will allow for the development of a more coherent understanding of KIE, how impact is created through KIE and how policy implication can be targeted to specific aspects of KIE.

NOTE

1. We would like to acknowledge Marcus Perkmann, a researcher at Imperial College. His review paper on academic engagement versus commercialization (Perkmann et al., 2013) was developed in parallel, and based upon a very similar methodology. We recommend that readers also review the methodology of that article, which was carried out on a different subject.

References

Aaboen, L. (2009), 'Explaining incubators using firm analogy', *Technovation*, **29** (10), 657–70.

AEGIS Survey (2012), www.aegis-fp7.eu.

Aldrich, H.E. and P.R. Reese (1993), 'Does networking pay off? A panel study of entrepreneurs in the research triangle', in N. Churchill (ed.), *Frontiers of Entrepreneurship Research*, Babson, MA: Babson College, pp. 325–99.

Aldrich, H.E and C. Zimmer (1986), 'Entrepreneurship through social networks', in D. Sexton and R. Smilor (eds), *The Art and Science of Entrepreneurship*, New York: Ballinger, pp. 3–23.

Anderson, A., J. Park and S. Jack (2007), 'Entrepreneurial social capital – conceptualizing social capital in new high-tech firms', *International Small Business Journal*, **25** (3), 245–72.

Antonelli, C. (1999), 'The evolution of the industrial organisation of the production of knowledge', *Cambridge Journal of Economics*, **23** (2), 243–60.

Ardichvili, A., R. Cardozo and S. Ray (2003), 'A theory of entrepreneurial opportunity identification and development', *Journal of Business Venturing*, **18** (1), 105–23.

Atherton, A. (2009), 'Rational actors, knowledgeable agents extending pecking order considerations of new venture financing to incorporate founder experience, knowledge and networks', *International Small Business Journal*, **27** (4), 470–95.

Avnimelech, G., D. Schwartz and R. Bar-El (2007), 'Entrepreneurial high-tech cluster development: Israel's experience with venture capital and technological incubators', *European Planning Studies*, **15** (9), 1181–98.

Bader, M.A. (2008), 'Managing intellectual property in inter-firm R&D collaborations in knowledge-intensive industries', *International Journal of Technology Management*, **41** (3–4), 311–35.

Bagchi-Sen, S. (2007), 'Strategic considerations for innovation and commercialization in the US biotechnology sector', *European Planning Studies*, **15** (6), 753–66.

Baldini, N. (2006), 'University patenting and licensing activity: a review of the literature', *Research Evaluation*, **15** (3), 197–207.

Bates, T. (1997), *Race, Upward Mobility, and Self-employment: An Illusive American Dream*, Baltimore, MD: Johns Hopkins University Press.

Baum, A.C., T. Calabrese and B.S. Silverman (2000), 'Don't go it alone: alliance network composition and startups' performance in Canadian biotechnology', *Strategic Management Journal*, **21**, 267–94.

Bayazit, N. (2004), 'Investigating design: a review of forty years of design research', *Design Issues*, **20** (1), 16–29.

Beckman, S.L. and M. Barry (2007), 'Innovation as a learning process: embedded design thinking', *California Management Review*, **50** (1), 25–56.

Bell, J., D. Crick and S. Young (2004), 'Small firm internationalization and business strategy – an exploratory study of "knowledge-intensive" and "traditional" manufacturing firms in the UK', *International Small Business Journal*, **22** (1), 23–56.

Ben-Ari, G. and N.S. Vonortas (2007), 'Risk financing for knowledge-based enterprises: mechanisms and policy options', *Science and Public Policy*, **34** (7), 475–88.

Berry, M.M.J. (1996), 'Technical entrepreneurship, strategic awareness and corporate transformation in small high-tech firms', *Technovation*, **16** (9), 487–98.

Bourelos, E., M. Magnusson and M. McKelvey (2012), 'Investigating the complexity facing academic entrepreneurs in science and engineering: the complementarities of research performance, networks and support structures in commercialization', *Cambridge Journal of Economics*, **36**, 751–80.

Bousbaci, R. (2008), '"Models of man" in design thinking: the "bounded rationality" episode', *Design Issues*, **24** (4), 38–52.

Braha, D. and O. Maimon (1997), 'The design process: properties, paradigms, and structure', *Systems, Man and Cybernetics, Part A: Systems and Humans, IEEE Transactions*, **27** (2), 146–66.

Brass, D.J. (1984), 'Being in the right place: a structural analysis of individual influence in an organization', *Administrative Science Quarterly*, **29**, 518–39.

Brass, D.J. (1992), 'Power in organizations: a social network perspective', in G. Moore and J.A. Whitt (eds), *Research in Politics and Society*, Greenwich, CT: Westview Press, pp. 295–323.

Braunerhjelm, P., Z. Acs, D. Audretsch and B. Carlsson (2010), 'The missing link: knowledge diffusion and entrepreneurship in endogenous growth', *Small Business Economics*, **34**, 105–25.

Breschi, S., F. Malerba and L. Orsenigo (2000), 'Technological regimes and Schumpeterian patterns of innovation', *Economic Journal*, **110**, 388–410.

Broberg, O., A. Axelsson and G. Sjöblom (2013). 'Entrepreneurial exploitation of creative destruction and the ambiguity of knowledge in the emerging field of digital advertising' in M. McKelvey and A.H. Lassen, *How Entrepreneurs Do What They Do*, Cheltenham, UK, and Northampton, MA, USA: Edward Elgar.

Brockhaus, R.H. Sr (1980), 'Risk taking propensity of entrepreneurs', *Academy of Management Journal*, **23** (3), 509–20.

Brody, P. and D. Ehrlich (1998), 'Can big companies become successful venture capitalists?', *McKinsey Quarterly*, **2**, 51–63.

Brown, B. and J.E. Butler (1995), 'Competitors as allies: a study of entrepreneurial networks in the U.S. wine industry', *Journal of Small Business Management*, **33** (3), 57–66.

Brown, T. (2008), 'Design thinking', *Harvard Business Review*, June, 1–10.

Bruderl, J. and R. Schussler (1990), 'Organizational mortality: the liabilities of newness and adolescence', *Administrative Science Quarterly*, **35** (3), 530–47.

Brush, C.G. and P.A. Vanderwerf (1992), 'A comparison of methods and sources for obtaining estimates of new ventures performance', *Journal of Business Venturing*, **7** (2), 157–70.

Buchanan, R. (1992), 'Wicked problems in design thinking', *Design Issues*, **8** (2), 5–21.

Buchanan, R. (1995), 'Wicked problems in design thinking' in V. Margolin and R. Buchanan (eds), *The Idea of Design, A Design Issues Reader*, Cambridge, MA: MIT Press, pp. 3–29.

Camerer, C. and D. Lovallo (1999), 'Overconfidence and excess entry: an experimental approach', *American Economic Review*, **89** (1), 306–18.

Capaldo, A. (2007), 'Network structure and innovation: the leveraging of a dual network as a distinctive relational capability', *Strategic Management Journal*, **28** (6), 585–608.

Carlsson, B., P. Braunerhjelm, M. McKelvey, C. Olofsson, L. Persson and H. Ylinenpää (2012), 'The evolving domain of entrepreneurship research', paper presented at the International Joseph A. Schumpeter Society, July, Brisbane, Australia.

Cassiman, B. and E. Veugelers (2006), 'In search of complementarity in innovation strategy: internal R&D and external knowledge acquisition', *Management Science*, **52** (1), 68–82.

Casson, P.D. and T.M. Nisar (2007), 'Entrepreneurship and organizational design: investor specialization', *Management Decision*, **45** (5), 883–96.

Chandler, G.N. and E. Jansen (1992), 'The founder self-assessed competence and venture performance,' *Journal of Business Venturing*, **7** (3), 223–36.

Chesbrough, H. (2000), 'Designing corporate ventures in the shadow of private venture capital', *California Management Review*, **42** (3), 31–49.

Chesbrough, H. (2003), *Open Innovation: The New Imperative for Creating and Profiting from Technology*, Cambridge, MA: Harvard Business Press.

Chesbrough, H. and S. Socolof (2003), 'Sustaining venture creation from industrial laboratories', *Research-Technology Management*, **46** (4), 16–19.

Chetty, S.K. and H.J.M. Wilson (2003), 'Collaborating with competitors to acquire resources', *International Business Review*, **12** (1), 61–81.

Christensen, C.M. and M.E. Raynor (2003), 'Why hard-nosed executives should care about management theory', *Harvard Business Review*, **81** (9), 66–74.

Clausen, C. and Y. Yoshinaka (2007), 'Staging socio-technical spaces: translating across boundaries in design', *Journal of Design Research*, **6** (1), 61–78.

Cockburn, I.M. and R.M. Henderson (1998), 'Absorptive capacity, coauthoring behavior, and the organization of research in drug discovery', *Journal of Industrial Economics*, **46**, 157–82.

Cohen, W.M. and D.A. Levinthal (1990), 'Absorptive capacity: a new perspective on learning and innovation', *Administrative Science Quarterly*, **35** (1), 128–52.

Cook, S.D.N. and J.S. Brown (1999), 'Bridging epistemologies: the generative dance between organizational knowledge and organizational knowing', *Organization Science*, **10** (4), 381–400.

Coviello, N.E. (2006), 'The network dynamics of international new ventures', *Journal of International Business Studies*, **37**, 713–31.

Covin, J.G. and M.P. Miles (2007), 'Strategic use of corporate venturing', *Entrepreneurship Theory and Practice*, **31** (2), 183–207.

Crick, D. (2009), 'The internationalisation of born global and international new venture SMEs', *International Marketing Review*, **26** (4/5), 453–76.

Crilly, N. (2010), 'The structure of design revolutions: Kuhnian paradigm shifts in creative problem solving', *Design Issues*, **26** (1), 54–66.

Cross, N. (1997), 'Creativity in design: analyzing and modeling the creativity leap', *Leonardo*, 30 (4), 311–17.

Dahlstrand, A.L. (1997), 'Entrepreneurial spin-off enterprises in Goteborg, Sweden', *European Planning Studies*, **5** (5), 659.

Das, T.K. and B. Teng (1998), 'Between trust and control: developing confidence in partner cooperation in alliances', *Academy of Management Review*, **23** (3), 491–512.

Davidsson, P., M.B. Low and M. Wright (2001), 'Editors' introduction: Low and MacMillan ten years on: achievements and future directions for entrepreneurship research', *Entrepreneurship Theory and Practice*, **25** (4), 5–16.

De Bono, E. (1978), *Opportunities: A Handbook of Business Opportunity Search*, Ringwood, VIC: Penguin Books Australia.

De Carolis, D.M., B.E. Litzky and K.A. Eddleston (2009), 'Why networks enhance the progress of new venture creation: the influence of social capital and cognition', *Entrepreneurship Theory and Practice*, **33** (2), 527–45.

De Clercq, D. and P. Arenius (2006), 'The role of knowledge in business start-up activity', *International Small Business Journal*, **24** (4), 339–58.

Deeds, D.L., P.Y. Mang and M. Frandsen (1997), 'The quest for legitimacy: a study of biotechnology IPOs', *Frontiers of Entrepreneurship Research*, Wellesley, MA: Center for Entrepreneurial Studies, pp. 533–43.

Deiaco, E., A. Hughes and M. McKelvey (2012), 'Universities as strategic actors in the knowledge economy', *Cambridge Journal of Economics*, **36**, 525–41.

Dittmar, A. (2004), 'Capital structure in corporate spin-offs', *Journal of Business*, **77** (1), 9–43.

Dorst, K. (2006), 'Design problems and design paradoxes', *Design Issues*, **22** (3), 4–17.

Dorst, K. and N. Cross (2001), 'Creativity in the design process: co-evolution of problem–solution', *Design Studies*, **22** (5), 425–37.

Eckhardt, J.T. and S.A. Shane (2003), 'Opportunities and entrepreneurship', *Journal of Management*, **29**, 333–49.

Fan, T. and P. Phan (2007), 'International new ventures: revisiting the influences behind the "born-global" firm', *Journal of International Business Studies*, **38**, 1113–31.

Faulkner, D. and G. Johnson (1992), *The Challenge of Strategic Management*, London: Kogan Page.

Feldman, J.M. and M. Klofsten (2000), 'Medium-sized firms and the limits to growth: a case study in the evolution of a spin-off firm', *European Planning Studies*, **8** (5), 631–50.

Freeman, J. (1999), 'Venture capital as an economy of time', in R.T.A.J. Leenders and S.M. Gabbay (eds), *Corporate Social Capital and Liability*, Boston, MA: Kluwer Academic Publishing, pp. 460–82.

Garavaglia, C. and D. Grieco (2005), 'Hand in hand with entrepreneurship: a critical overview from entrepreneurship to knowledge-based entrepreneurship', paper presented at Knowledge-based Entrepreneurship: Innovation, Networks and Systems (KEINS), Milan.

Garcia-Quevedo, J. and F. Mas-Verdu (2008), 'Does only size matter in the use of knowledge intensive services?', *Small Business Economics*, **31** (2), 137–46.

Gartner, W.B. (1985), 'A conceptual framework for describing the phenomenon of new venture creation', *Academy of Management Review*, **10** (4), 696–706.

Gartner, W.B. (1993), 'Words lead to deeds: towards an organizational emergence vocabulary', *Journal of Business Venturing*, **8** (3), 231–9.

Gatewood, E.J., K.G. Shaver and W.B. Gartner (1995), 'A longitudinal study of cognitive factors influencing start-up behavior and success at venture creation', *Journal of Business Venturing*, **10** (5), 371–91.

Goel, S. and R. Karri (2006), 'Entrepreneurs, effectual logic, and over-trust', *Entrepreneurship Theory and Practice*, **30** (4), 477–93.

Gompers, P.A. and J. Lerner (1998), 'Venture capital distributions: short- and long-run reactions', *Journal of Finance*, **53**, December, 2161–83.

Grady, J. (1996), 'The scope of visual sociology', *Visual Sociology*, **11** (2), 10–24.

Granovetter, M. (1973), 'The strength of weak ties', *American Journal of Sociology*, **78**, 1360–80.

Grimaldi, R. and A. Grandi (2005), 'Business incubators and new venture creation: an assessment of incubating models', *Technovation*, **25** (2), 111–21.

Groen, A.J., I.A.M. Wakkee and P.C. De Weerd-Nederhof (2008), 'Managing tensions in a high-tech start-up – an innovation journey in social system perspective', *International Small Business Journal*, **26** (1), 57–81.

Gupta, P. (2004), *The Role of Board Members in Venture Capital Backed Companies: Rules, Responsibilities and Motivations of Board Members – From Management & VC Perspective,* Boston, MA: Aspatore Books.

Hamel, G. and C.K. Prahalad (1989), 'Strategic intent', *Harvard Business Review*, **83** (7), 148–61.

Hannan, M.T. and J. Freeman (1984), 'Structural inertia and organizational change', *American Sociological Review*, **49**, 149–64.

Hansen, E.L. (1995), 'Entrepreneurial networks and new organization growth', *Entrepreneurship Theory and Practice*, **19** (4), 7–19.

Hayek, F.A. (1945), 'The use of knowledge in society', *American Economic Review*, **35** (4), 519–30.

Heidenreich, M. (2009), 'Innovation patterns and location of European low- and medium-technology industries', *Research Policy*, **38** (3), 483–94.

Hellmann, T. (2007), 'Entrepreneurs and the process of obtaining resources', *Journal of Economics and Management Strategy*, **16** (1), 81–109.

Heneman, H.G. and R.A. Berkley (1999), 'Applicant attraction practices and outcomes among small businesses', *Journal of Small Business Management*, **37** (1), 53–74.

Higgins, M.C. and R. Gulati (2000), 'Getting off to a good start: the effects of top management team affiliations on prestige of investment bank and IPO success', Harvard University working paper, Cambridge, MA.

Hite, J.M. (2000), 'Patterns of multidimensionality in embedded network ties of emerging entrepreneurial firms', paper presented at the annual meeting of the Academy of Management, Toronto, Canada.

Hoang, H. and N. Young (2000), 'Social embeddedness and entrepreneurial opportunity recognition; (more) evidence of embeddedness', Babson College working paper, Babson, MA.

Holmén, M., M. Magnusson and M. McKelvey (2007), 'What are innovative opportunities?', *Industry and Innovation*, **14** (1), 27–45.

Hornsby, J.S. and D.F. Kuratko (1990), 'Human resource management in small business: critical issues for the 1990s', *Journal of Small Business Management*, **28** (3), 9–18.

Hsu, D.H., E.B. Roberts and C.E. Eesley (2007), 'Entrepreneurs from technology-based universities: evidence from MIT', *Research Policy*, **36** (5), 768–88.

Huse, M. (2007), *Boards, Governance and Value Creation: The Human Side of Corporate Governance*, Cambridge: Cambridge University Press.

Huss, W.R. and E.J. Honton (1987), 'Scenario planning: what style should you use?', *Long Range Planning*, **20** (4), 21–9.

Jacobsen, A. and A.H. Lassen (2012), 'User-driven innovation in business networks: a literature review', paper presented at the conference Innovation in Business Networks, Kolding, Denmark, 22–23 March.

Jarillo, C.J. (1988), 'On strategic networks', *Strategic Management Journal*, **9**, 31–41.

Jennings, P. and G. Beaver (1997), 'The performance and competitive advantage of small firms: a management perspective', *International Small Business Journal*, **15**, 63–75.

Johannisson, B., O. Alexanderson, K. Nowicki and K. Senneseth (1994), 'Beyond anarchy and organization: entrepreneurs in contextual networks', *Entrepreneurship Regional Development*, **6**, 329–56.

Jones, C., W.S. Hesterly and S.P. Borgatti (1997), 'A general theory of network governance: exchange conditions and social mechanisms', *Academy of Management Review*, **22** (4), 911–45.

Kahneman, D. and A. Tversky (1982), 'The psychology of preferences', *Scientific American*, **246** (1), 160–73.

Kahneman, D., P. Slovic and A. Tversky (1982), *Judgement under Uncertainty: Heuristics and Biases*, Cambridge: Cambridge University Press.

Katila, R. (1997), 'Technology strategies for growth and innovation: a study of biotechnology ventures', *Frontiers of Entrepreneurship Research*, Wellesley, MA: Center for Entrepreneurial Studies, pp. 405–18.

Katila, R. and P.Y. Mang (1999), *Interorganizational Development Activities: The Likelihood and Timing of Contracts*, Academy of Management Proceedings, Chicago, IL: Academy of Management.

Keeble, D. and R. Oakey (1998), 'Spatial variations in innovation in high-technology small and medium-sized enterprises: a review', in A. Cosh and A. Hughes (eds), *Innovation: National Policies, Legal Perspectives and the Role of Smaller Firms*, Cheltenham, UK and Lyme, NH, USA: Edward Elgar.

Kirzner, I.M. (1973), *Competition and Entrepreneurship*, Chicago, IL: University of Chicago Press.

Kirzner, I.M. (1982), 'The theory of entrepreneurship in economic growth', in C.A. Kent, D.L. Sexton and K.H. Vesper (eds), *Encyclopedia of Entrepreneurship*, Englewood Cliffs, NJ: Prentice-Hall, pp. 272–6.

Klayman, J., B. Soll, C. González-Vallejo and S. Barlas (1999), 'Overconfidence: it depends on how, what, and whom you ask', *Organizational Behavior and Human Decision Processes*, **79** (3), 216–47.

Klofsten, M. and D. Jones-Evans (2000), 'Comparing academic entrepreneurship in Europe – the case of Sweden and Ireland', *Small Business Economics*, **14** (4), 299–309.

Knight, G., T.K. Madsen and P. Servais (2004), 'An inquiry into born-global firms in Europe and the USA', *International Marketing Review*, **21** (6), 645–65.

Krackhardt, D. (1990), 'Assessing the political landscape: structure, cognition, and power in networks', *Administrative Science Quarterly*, **35**, 342–69.

Krackhardt, D. (1995), 'Entrepreneurial opportunities in an entrepreneurial firm: a structural approach', *Entrepreneurship Theory Practice*, **19**, 53–69.

Landström, H. (2007), *Handbook of Research on Venture Capital*, Cheltenham, UK and Northampton, MA, USA: Edward Elgar.

Larson, A. (1992), 'Network dyads in entrepreneurial settings: a study of the governance of exchange relations', *Administrative Science Quarterly*, **37**, 76–104.

Lassen, A.H. (2013) "How tensions between exploration and exploitation drives the development process of KIE: the case of Sensor Inc.", in M. McKelvey and A.H. Lassen, *How Entrepreneurs Do What They Do*, Cheltenham, UK, and Northampton, MA, USA: Edward Elgar.

Lassen, A.H., M. McKelvey and D. Slepniov (2012), 'Strategies for international development in knowledge intensive new ventures: implications for Asian-European collaboration', paper presented at the 28th Annual Euro-Asia Management Studies Association Conference, Strategies of International Development in Euro-Asian Business, University of Gothenburg, Gothenburg, Sweden.

Lawson, B. (1980), *How Designers Think: The Design Process Demystified*, 4th edn, Burlington, MA: Elsevier.

Lerner, J. (2009), *Boulevard of Broken Dreams: Why Public Efforts to Boost Entrepreneurship and Venture Capital have Failed – and What to Do About It*, Princeton, NJ: Princeton University Press.

Lichtenstein, B.B., K.J. Dooley and G.T. Lumpkin (2006), 'Measuring emergence in the dynamics of new venture creation', *Journal of Business Venturing*, **21** (2), 153–75.

Lichtenthaler, U. and E. Lichtenthaler (2009), 'A capability-based framework for open innovation: complementing absorptive capacity', *Journal of Management Studies*, **46**, 1315–38.

Lindberg, T., C. Meinel and R. Wagner (2011), 'Design thinking: a fruitful concept for IT development?', in C. Meinel, L. Leifer and H. Plattner (eds), *Design Thinking: Understand, Improve, Apply*, Berlin and Heidelberg, Germany: Springer, pp. 3–16.

Lissoni, F., P. Llerena, M. McKelvey and B. Sanditov (2008), 'Academic patenting in Europe: new evidence from the KEINS database', *Research Evaluation*, **17** (2), 87–102.

Lorenzoni, G. and A. Lipparini (1999), 'The leveraging of interfirm relationships as a distinctive organizational capability: a longitudinal study', *Strategic Management Journal*, **20** (4), 317–38.

Malerba, F. and M. McKelvey (2010), 'Conceptualizing knowledge intensive entrepreneurship: concepts and models', paper presented at DIME – AEGIS – LIEE/NTUA 2010 Conference, The Emergence and Growth of Knowledge Intensive Entrepreneurship in a Comparative Perspective. Studying Various Aspects in Different Contexts, 29–30 April, Athens.

March, J.G. (1991), 'Exploration and exploitation in organizational learning', *Organization Science*, **2** (1), 71–87.

Maula, M. and G. Murray (2000), 'Corporate venture capital and the creation of US public companies: the impact of sources of venture capital on the performance of portfolio companies', in M. Hitt, R. Amit, C.E. Lucier and R.D. Nixon (eds), *Creating Value: Winners in the New Business Environment*, Oxford: Wiley-Blackwell, pp. 164–87.

McClelland, D.C. (1961), *The Achieving Society*, Princeton, NJ: Van Nostrand.

McDougall, P. P. and B.M. Oviatt (2000), 'International entrepreneurship: the intersection of two research paths', *Academy of Management Journal*, **43** (5), 902–6.

McEvily, B. and A. Zaheer (1999), 'Bridging ties: a source of firm heterogeneity in competitive capabilities', *Strategic Management Journal*, **20**, 1133–56.

McKelvey, M. (1996), *Evolutionary Innovations: The Business of Biotechnology*, New York: Oxford University Press.

McKelvey, M. and M. Holmèn (2006), *Flexibility and Stability in the Innovating Economy*, Oxford: Oxford University Press.

McKelvey, M. and M. Holmèn (2008), *Learning to Compete in European Universities: From Social Institutions to Knowledge Businesses*, Cheltenham, UK and Northampton, MA, USA: Edward Elgar.

McKelvey, M. and A.H. Lassen (2013), *How Entrepreneurs Do What They Do: Case Studies of Knowledge Intensive Entrepreneurship*, Cheltenham, UK and Northampton, MA, USA: Edward Elgar.

McKelvey, M., D. Ljungberg and A.H. Lassen (2012), 'Case study analysis in AEGIS', available at www.aegis-fp7.eu.

McKelvey, M., D. Ljungberg and J. Laage-Hellman (2013), 'Collaborative research in innovative food: an example of renewing a traditional low-tech industry', in M. McKelvey and A.H. Lassen, *How Entrepreneurs Do What They Do*, Cheltenham, UK, and Northampton, MA, USA: Edward Elgar.

Metrick, A. (2006), *Venture Capital and the Finance of Innovation*, Hoboken, NJ: John Wiley & Sons.

Moenaert, R.K., F. Caeldries, A. Lievens and E. Wauters (2000), 'Communication flows in international product innovation teams', *Journal of Product Innovation Management*, **17**, 360–77.

Nicholls-Nixon, C.L. (2005), 'Rapid growth and high performance: the entrepreneur's "impossible dream"?', *Academy of Management Executive*, **19** (1), 77–89.

Nielsen, S.L., A.H. Lassen, L.M. Nielsen and M. Mikkelsen (2012), 'Opportunity design: understanding entrepreneurial opportunities through design thinking', *International Journal of Entrepreneurial Behaviour and Research*, forthcoming.

Oestergaard, C. and E. Park (2013), 'Knowledge intensive entrepreneurship from firm exit in a high-tech cluster: the case of the wireless communications cluster in Aalborg, Denmark', in M. McKelvey and A.H. Lassen, *How Entrepreneurs Do What They Do*, Cheltenham, UK, and Northampton, MA, USA: Edward Elgar.

Orlikowski, W.J. (2004), 'Managing and designing: attending to reflexiveness and enactment', in R.J. Boland and F. Collopy (eds), *Managing and Designing*, Stanford, CA: University of Stanford Press, pp. 85–90.

Parhankangas, A. and P. Arenius (2003), 'From a corporate venture to an independent company: a base for a taxonomy for corporate spin-off firms', *Research Policy*, **32** (3), 463–81.

Park, J.S. (2005), 'Opportunity recognition and product innovation in entrepreneurial hi-tech start-ups: a new perspective and supporting case study', *Technovation*, **25** (7), 739–52.

Parker, S. (2004), *The Economics of Self-employment and Entrepreneurship*, Cambridge: Cambridge University Press.

Pavitt, K. (1984), 'Sectoral patterns of technical change: towards a taxonomy and a theory', *Research Policy*, **13** (6), 343–73.

Penrose, E.T. (1959), *The Theory of the Growth of the Firm*, New York: Oxford University Press.

Perkmann, M., V. Tartari, M. McKelvey et al. (2013), 'Academic engagement and commercialization; a review of the literature on university relations with industry', *Research Policy*, forthcoming.

Pirnay, F., B. Surlemont and F. Nlemvo (2003), 'Toward a typology of university spin-offs', *Small Business Economics*, **21** (4), 355–69.

Portes, A. and J. Sensenbrenner (1993), 'Embeddedness and immigration: notes on the social determinants of economic action', *American Journal of Sociology*, **98**, 1320–50.

Powell, W.W. (1990), 'Neither market nor hierarchy: network forms of organization', in L.L. Cummings and B.M. Staw (eds), *Research in Organizational Behavior*, vol. 12, Greenwich, CT: JAJ Press, pp. 295–336.

Pruitt, D.G. (1981), *Negotiation Behavior*, New York: Academic Press.

Rae, D. (2006), 'Entrepreneurial learning: a conceptual framework for technology-based enterprise', *Technology Analysis and Strategic Management*, **18** (1), 39–56.

Ranger-Moore, J. (1997), 'Bigger may be better, but is older wiser? Organizational age and size in the New York life insurance industry', *American Sociological Review*, **62** (6), 903–20.

Rindfleisch, A. and C. Moorman (2001), 'The acquesition and utilization of information in new product alliances: a strength-of-ties perspectives', *Journal of Marketing*, **65**, April, 1–18.

Rittel, H. (1972), 'On the planning crisis: systems analysis of the "first and second generations"', *Bedriftsøkonomen*, **8**, 390–6.

Rocha, F. (1997), 'Inter-firm technological cooperation: effects of absorptive capacity, firm-size and specialization', edition 9707 of UNU/INTECH discussion papers.

Roos, J., B. Victor and M. Statler (2004), 'Playing seriously with strategy', *Long Range Planning*, **37** (6), 549–68.

Rotter, J.B. (1975), 'Some problems and misconceptions related to the construct of internal versus external control of reinforcement', *Journal of Consulting and Clinical Psychology*, **43** (1), 56–67.

Ryhammar, L. and C. Brolin (1999), 'Creativity research: historical considerations and main lines of development', *Scandinavian Journal of Educational Research*, **43** (3), 259–73.

Said, R. and J. Roos (2002), 'Committing to strategy', Imagination Lab Foundation working paper series no. 15.

Salter, A.J. and B.R. Martin (2001), 'The economic benefits of publicly funded basic research: a critical review', *Research Policy*, **30**, 509–32.

Sapienza, H.J., A. Parhankangas and E. Autio (2004), 'Knowledge relatedness and post-spin-off growth', *Journal of Business Venturing*, **19** (6), 809–29.

Sarason, Y., T. Dean and J.F. Dillard (2006), 'Entrepreneurship as the nexus of individual and opportunity: a structuration view', *Journal of Business Venturing*, **21** (3), 286–305.

Sarasvathy, S.D. (2001), 'Causation and effectuation: toward a theoretical shift from economic inevitability to entrepreneurial contingency', *Academy of Management Review*, **26** (2), 243–63.

Sarasvathy, S. (2008), *Effectuation: Elements of Entrepreneurial Expertise*, Cheltenham, UK and Northampton, MA, USA: Edward Elgar.

Saxenian, A. (1991), 'The origins and dynamics of production networks in Silicon Valley', *Research Policy*, **20** (5), 423–37.

Scherer, F.M. (1965), 'Firm size, market structure, opportunity, and the output of patented inventions', *American Economic Review*, **55** (5), 1097–125.

Schumpeter, J. (1934), *The Theory of Economic Development*, Cambridge, MA: Harvard University Press.

Schwartz, P. (1991), *The Art of the Long View*, New York: Doubleday/Currency.

Sebastian, R. (2005), 'The interface between design and management', *Design Issues*, **21** (1), 81–91.

Shane, S.A. (2003), *A General Theory of Entrepreneurship: The Individual-opportunity Nexus*, Cheltenham, UK and Northampton, MA, USA: Edward Elgar.

Shane, S. (2009), 'Why encouraging more people to become entrepreneurs is bad public policy', *Small Business Economics*, **33**, 141–9.

Shane, S. and D. Cable (2002), 'Network ties, reputation, and the financing of new ventures', *Management Science*, **48** (3), 364–81.

Shane, S. and S. Venkataraman (2000), 'The promise of entrepreneurship as a field of research', *Academy of Management Review*, **25** (1), 217–26.

Simon, H.A. (1969), *Sciences of the Artificial*, Cambridge, MA: MIT Press.

Singh, R.P., G.E. Hills, G.T. Lumpkin and R.C. Hybels (1999), 'The entrepreneurial opportunity recognition process: examining the role of self-perceived alertness and social networks', paper presented at the 1999 Academy of Management Meeting, Chicago, IL.

Smeltzer, L.R., B.L. Van Hook and R.W. Hutt (1991), 'Analysis and use of advisors as information sources in venture startups', *Journal of Small Business Management*, **29** (3), 10–20.

Starr, J.A. and I.C. Macmillan (1990), 'Resource cooptation via social contracting: resource acquisition strategies for new ventures', *Strategic Management Journal*, **11**, 79–92.

Steinmueller, E. (2011), 'Social consequences of entrepreneurial activity and opportunities for European knowledge based societies', AEGIS WP3.2, available at www.aegis-fp7.eu.

Stinchcombe, A. (1965), 'Social structures and organizations', in J.G. March (ed.), *Handbook of Organizations*, Chicago, IL: Rand McNally, pp. 142–93.

Storey, D.J. (1982), *Entrepreneurship and the Small Firm*, London: Croom Helm.

Stuart, T.E., H. Hoang and R. Hybels (1999), 'Interorganizational endorsements and the performance of entrepreneurial ventures', *Administrative Science Quarterly*, **44** (2), 315–49.

Swann, C. (2002), 'Action research and the practice of design', *Design Issues*, **18** (1), 49–61.

Sykes, H.B. and Z. Block (1989), 'Corporate venturing obstacles – sources and solutions', *Journal of Business Venturing*, **4** (3), 159–67.

Teece, D.J., G. Pisano and A. Shuen (1997), 'Dynamic capabilities and strategic management', *Strategic Management Journal*, **18** (7), 509–33.

Thorelli, H.B (1986), 'Networks: between markets and hierarchies', *Strategic Management Journal*, **7**, 37–51.

Thurik, A.R. (1999), 'Entrepreneurship, industrial transformation and growth', in G.D. Libecap (ed.), *The Sources of Entrepreneurial Activity: Vol. 11, Advances in the Study of Entrepreneurship, Innovation, and Economic Growth*, Stamford, CT: JAI Press, pp. 29–65.

Todtling, F., P. Lehner and M. Trippl (2006), 'Innovation in knowledge intensive industries: the nature and geography of knowledge links', *European Planning Studies*, **14** (8), 1035–58.

Utterback, J.M. and G. Reitberger (1982), *Technology and Industrial Innovation in Sweden – A Study of New Technology-based Firms*, report submitted to the National Swedish Board for Technical Development (STU), Stockholm.

Vaghely, I.P. and P.-A. Julien (2010), 'Are opportunities recognized or constructed?: an information perspective on entrepreneurial opportunity identification', *Journal of Business Venturing*, **25** (1), 73–86.

Van de Ven, A.H., R. Hudson and D.M. Schroeder (1984), 'Designing new business startups: entrepreneurial, organizational, and ecological considerations', *Journal of Management*, **10** (1), Spring, 87–108.

van Leeuwen, T. and C. Jewitt (eds) (2000), *Handbook of Visual Analysis*, London: Sage Publications.

Vecchio, R.P. (2003), 'In search of gender advantage', *Leadership Quarterly*, **14**, 835–50.

Venkataraman, S. (1997), 'The distinctive domain of entrepreneurship research', in J. Katz (ed.), *Advances in Entrepreneurship, Firm Emergence and Growth*, vol. 3, Greenwich, CT: JAI Press, pp. 119–38.

von Hippel, E. (1988), *The Sources of Innovation*, New York: Oxford University Press.

Witt, U. (1998), 'Imagination and leadership – the neglected dimension of an evolutionary theory of the firm', *Journal of Economic Behavior and Organization*, **35** (2), 161–77.

Zahra, S.A. and G. George (2002), 'Absorptive capacity: a review, reconceptualization, and extension', *Academy of Management Review*, **27** (2), 185–203.

Index